American Pit Bull Terrier

By Steve Visuddhidham

Breeders' Best
A KENNEL CLUB BOOK™

AMERICAN PIT BULL TERRIER

ISBN: 1-59378-909-2

Copyright © 2004

Kennel Club Books, LLC
308 Main Street, Allenhurst, NJ 07711 USA
Printed in South Korea

ALL RIGHTS RESERVED. NO PART OF THIS BOOK MAY BE REPRODUCED IN ANY FORM, BY PHOTOSTAT, SCANNER, MICROFILM, XEROGRAPHY OR ANY OTHER MEANS, OR INCORPORATED INTO ANY INFORMATION RETRIEVAL SYSTEM, ELECTRONIC OR MECHANICAL, WITHOUT THE WRITTEN PERMISSION OF THE COPYRIGHT OWNER.

10 9 8 7 6 5 4 3 2

PHOTOS BY:
Bernd Brinkmann,
Isabelle Français and
Nancy Liguori.

DRAWINGS BY:
Yolyanko el Habanero.

Breeders' Best

Contents

- 4   Meet the American Pit Bull Terrier
- 12   Description of the APBT
- 20   Are You an APBT Person?
- 28   Selecting an APBT Breeder
- 32   Finding the Right APBT Puppy
- 40   Welcoming the APBT
- 48   House-training and More
- 52   Your APBT's Education
- 60   Home Care for Your APBT
- 66   Feeding Your APBT
- 72   Grooming Your APBT
- 76   Keeping Your APBT Active
- 84   Your APBT and His Vet
- 94   Your Aging APBT

CHAPTER 1

AMERICAN PIT BULL TERRIER

Meet the American Pit Bull Terrier

The American Pit Bull Terrier is a smart, agile, strong and very game dog. The word "game" in this context infers that the dog is so determined that he will never quit under any circumstances. He is popular in the United States even though he is not considered a purebred breed by the American Kennel Club. He can make a wonderful pet, and those who have successfully owned APBTs will swear by their loyalty, alertness, steady dispositions and ability to be loving members of the family. However, the

For all the tales that abound of the ferocious Pit Bull, he is actually quite a friendly dog, as shown by these smiling faces.

4

APBT is not the dog for everyone and, before purchasing this breed, you should do some reading, make some inquiries, meet some dogs and find a responsible breeder. A look at the history of the APBT will give the potential owner a good overview of the breed's background and why caution must be taken in the puppy search rather than purchasing the first puppy that you come across.

Today's APBT is far from his "all work" predecessors; the breed is quite full of play!

The American Pit Bull Terrier comes down from the fighting dogs of England and Ireland. Through the centuries, the baiting of animals (also called "blood sports") has been a popular, although extremely cruel, sport. Animals used for baiting were bulls, lions, cocks, dogs and, in Roman times, even man. Although the sport died out among the rich and royals, it remained an attractive pastime for the working people with little funds. One could breed a good fighting dog without any, or little, cost and make a

The breed's popularity and devotees span the globe. This handsome APBT hails from Germany.

American Pit Bull Terrier

week's salary in bets from a fight. In the 18th and 19th centuries, life was hard and little thought was given to the inhumanity of the sport. By the mid-1800s or so, bear and bull baiting were outlawed in Great Britain but dog fighting continued, particularly in the industrial areas of England. Eventually dog fighting was banned, but the sport continues underground to this day all over the world. Today gamblers, mafia and wreckless people who do not care about the breed stage dog fights for their own amusement and financial gain. Whenever a ring of dog fighters is found by the police, it is well reported in the newspapers and the general public finds it to be a despicable and inhumane sport.

The background of the APBT comes from the English and Irish pit-fighting dogs of the mid-19th century. At one time the APBT, the Staffordshire Bull Terrier and the American Staffordshire Terrier were considered to be the same breed. Originally these breeds came down from the English Bulldog and terrier breeds. The Bulldog, known as a fighting breed, was bred to a black and tan terrier or a white English Terrier to create a more agile and faster fighting dog. Over time, as the breeds were used for different purposes, they changed. Now they are three distinct breeds.

The American Staffordshire is the heaviest of the three dogs, and males will be 18 to 19 inches in height. Ears may be either cropped or uncropped, but the uncropped ear is preferred. The Staffordshire Bull Terrier is 14 to 16 inches in height and has an uncropped ear. The APBT may have cropped or uncropped ears and will weigh from 35 to 60 pounds for a male and 30 to 50 pounds for a female. No height specifications are set, so the APBT is seen in a range of sizes. He is one of the few

Meet the American Pit Bull Terrier

popular breeds that is not registered with the American Kennel Club. His two very close cousins, the Staffordshire Bull Terrier and the American Staffordshire Brown, in the *History of the American Pit Bull Terrier,* wrote extensively about the history of Pit Bulls in America. The history is long and complicated, but the

"Bull-and-terrier" breeds related to the APBT are, from left to right: the Bull Terrier, the American Staffordshire Terrier and the Staffordshire Bull Terrier.

Terrier, are both registered with the AKC.

Dogs of the PitBull/Staffordshire type were brought to America as early as the mid-1800s, and dogs continued for many years to be imported from both Ireland and England to American shores. Wayne D. names of the Irish dogs are surely compelling: Bob the Fool, Blind Buck, Morrow's Fly and Galvin's Pup. All of these dogs were bred for fighting, and the descendants of Bob the Fool were considered to be outstanding fighters. Imported English dogs had equally as colorful

American Pit Bull Terrier

CHAPTER 1

Fighting dogs' ears typically were cropped to give the opponent less to grab onto. APBTs today are seen either cropped or with natural ears, like this youngster, which contributes to a softer look.

Meet the American Pit Bull Terrier

names: Turk, Toby, Curley, Crib and Pilot; the latter was not only a powerful and winning fighter but also left a legacy through his excellent progeny.

with children. The APBT/Staffordshire Terrier was considered to be a symbol of American patriotism in the early 1900s. By 1936, with the advent of the *Our Gang*

APBT with cropped ears. Some owners prefer to keep the traditional cropped look even though their dogs are not used for fighting or working.

The APBT began to enjoy a surge of popularity in the United States. The breed was found to make wonderful pets, devoted, loyal and good movies with the "Lil' Rascals" and Pete the Pup, who was an APBT/AmStaff, the breed became very popular. It was at this time that the AKC

American Pit Bull Terrier

registered the breed as the Staffordshire Terrier.

In 1935, a group of individuals formed the Staffordshire Terrier Club of America with the hope of receiving recognition from the American Kennel Club. In 1936, APBTs and Staffordshire Terriers were both registered with the AKC although some APBT breeders registered their dogs with the American Dog Breeders Association (ADBA) and the United Kennel Club (UKC). As time went on, fewer APBTs were registered with the AKC and, by 1972, the Staffordshire Terrier was renamed the American Staffordshire Terrier. The UKC and the ADBA began holding their own shows for American Pit Bull Terriers.

From 1950 to the early 1970s, the breed became relatively obscure. A few breeders remained true, breeding good dogs with good pedigrees. By the 1980s, the breed once again started gaining in popularity, and individuals with little or no knowledge of the breed started breeding dogs with little consideration for pedigree or temperament. Many bred for exactly what the responsible breeders were *not* breeding for: human-aggressive dogs. Before long, articles about Pit Bulls' inflicting terrible wounds on children began appearing in the media. In addition, dog fighting once again began underground in rough neighborhoods, with tough owners pitting their dogs against one another. This caused more media attention and more problems for the APBT.

Owners of well-bred, well-trained APBTs maintain that the breed is wonderful with children. Of course, as with any breed, the children must be taught the proper way to handle a dog.

Meet the American Pit Bull Terrier

Breeders' Best

Today the breed struggles with its reputation as cities try to pass legislation against the APBT. For these reasons, it is absolutely essential that a prospective owner of an APBT does his homework, knows that this dog will be accepted in his neighborhood and purchases his dog from none other than a responsible breeder, one who has been breeding for some time, who breeds to the standard and does temperament testing on his dogs.

The APBT is a versatile, fun companion, ready to join in any game or activity with his owners.

MEET THE AMERICAN PIT BULL TERRIER

Overview

- The APBT's ancestry traces back to fighting dogs of Ireland and England that were used in cruel "baiting" and "blood sports."
- The APBT and closely related breeds derived from crosses between the Bulldog of yore and various terrier breeds.
- Although popular in the US, the APBT is not recognized by the AKC like his close relatives, the American Staffordshire Terrier and Staffordshire Bull Terrier. There are other large national registries to promote and protect the APBT.
- The APBT got a bad reputation with the resurgence of underground dog fighting and the rise in irresponsible breeders. Truly dedicated breeders are working hard to preserve the admirable qualities of the breed and overcome its negative image by breeding sound dogs that make wonderful pets.

CHAPTER 2

AMERICAN
PIT BULL TERRIER

Description of the APBT

Every breed of dog, whether registered with the American Kennel Club, United Kennel Club, American Dog Breeders Association or other registry, has a breed standard. This written standard gives a mental picture of how the breed should look, act and more.

For the American Pit Bull Terrier, the two main organizations that register the breed, the UKC and the ADBA, each have their own standard. The UKC standard is written in a format that is very similar

The APBT's chest has impressive width and musculature, and the legs should be straight and strong.

to that used by the AKC for its breeds, and the ADBA standard is written in a paragraph form.

Taking the UKC standard first, words denoting strength are used throughout: The shoulders are strong and muscular, the back is short and strong and the pasterns are reasonably strong. He should have well-pronounced jaws displaying strength, the neck is muscular and the thighs are long with muscles developed. Weight is not important, with males weighing between 35 to 60 pounds and females weighing from 30 to 50 pounds. Ears may be cropped or uncropped.

The breed is best known for its outstanding jaw strength, and APBTs enjoy games that utilize this trait. Owners must exercise caution, however, as the breed is very tenacious—once he latches onto something, he often won't let go.

The APBT's muscular neck widens as it blends smoothly into the shoulders.

The ADBA standard should be read, as this will certainly give a prospective owner of an APBT a very good idea of what the breed was originally bred for...the dog was bred

American Pit Bull Terrier

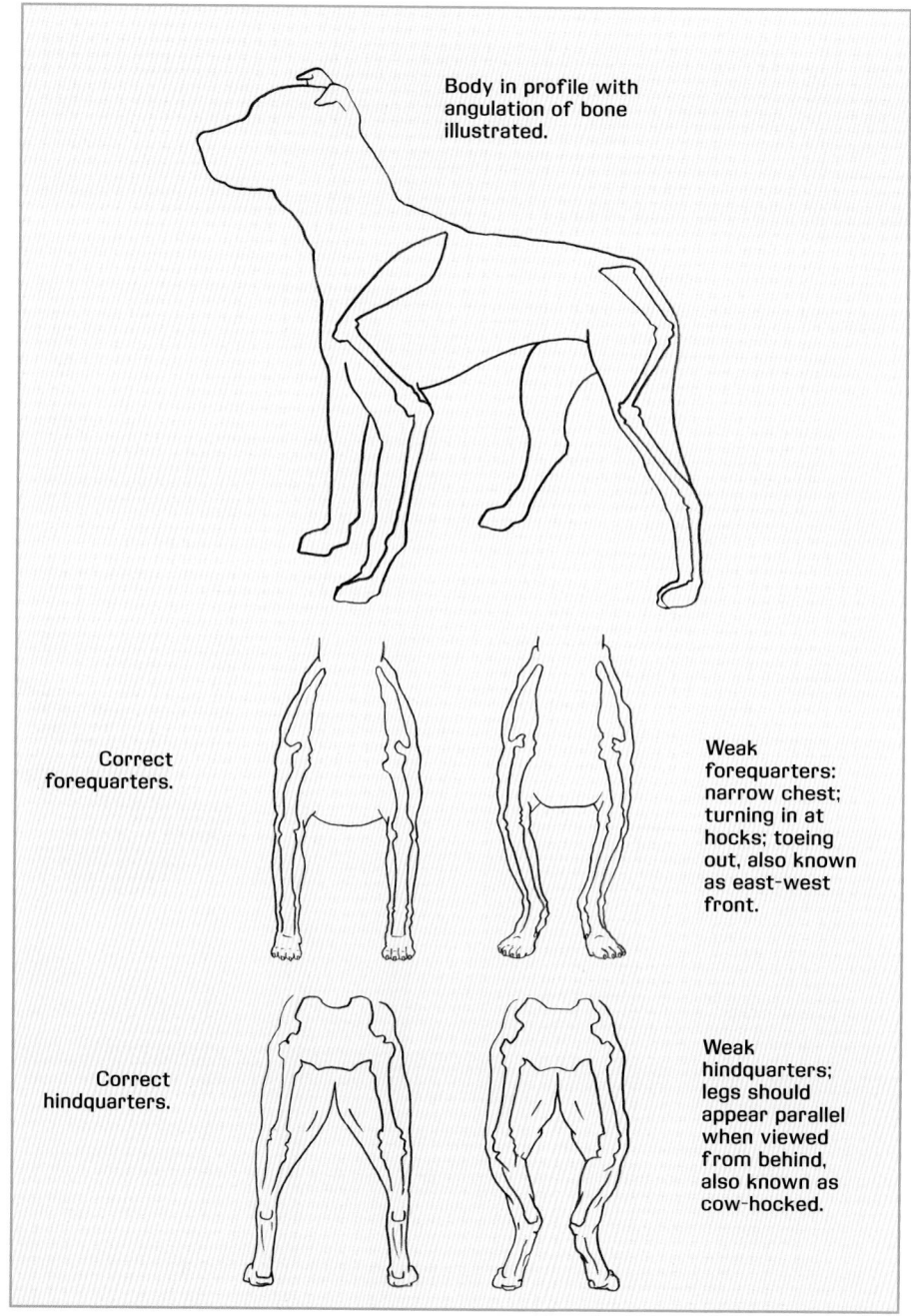

Description of the APBT

to win a fight. To some degree or another he was bred for gameness, attitude, stamina, wrestling ability and biting ability. The ADBA standard notes that this should be a dog that looks "square" in profile. Ears can be cropped or uncropped, and any coat color is acceptable.

The standard notes: "Above all, the American Pit Bull Terrier is an all-around athlete. His body is called on for speed, power, ability and stamina. He must be balanced in all directions. Too much of one thing robs him of another. He is not an entity formed according to human specialists. In his winning form he is a fighting machine...a thing of beauty." The breakdown of the standard on a 100-point scale is: Overall appearance–20 points; attitude of dog–10 points; head and neck–15 points; front end of dog–20 points; rear end of dog–30 points; tail and coat–5 points.

We have covered some of the negatives about the American Pit Bull Terrier, but there are many reasons why one would want to own this breed! A well-bred Pit Bull can be a joy to have as a pet. He is exceptionally athletic, very eager to please and affectionate, and he makes an excellent family dog. In courage, gameness and resolve, the breed is supreme. APBTs are stubborn enough to try to overcome any challenge. They have an extremely high pain threshold in addition to their rock-steady dispositions.

During the early 20th century, this was the breed used as a national symbol of courage and pride. They are not a guard dog, as a German Shepherd or a Doberman Pinscher would be, as the APBT has not been bred for guarding. If

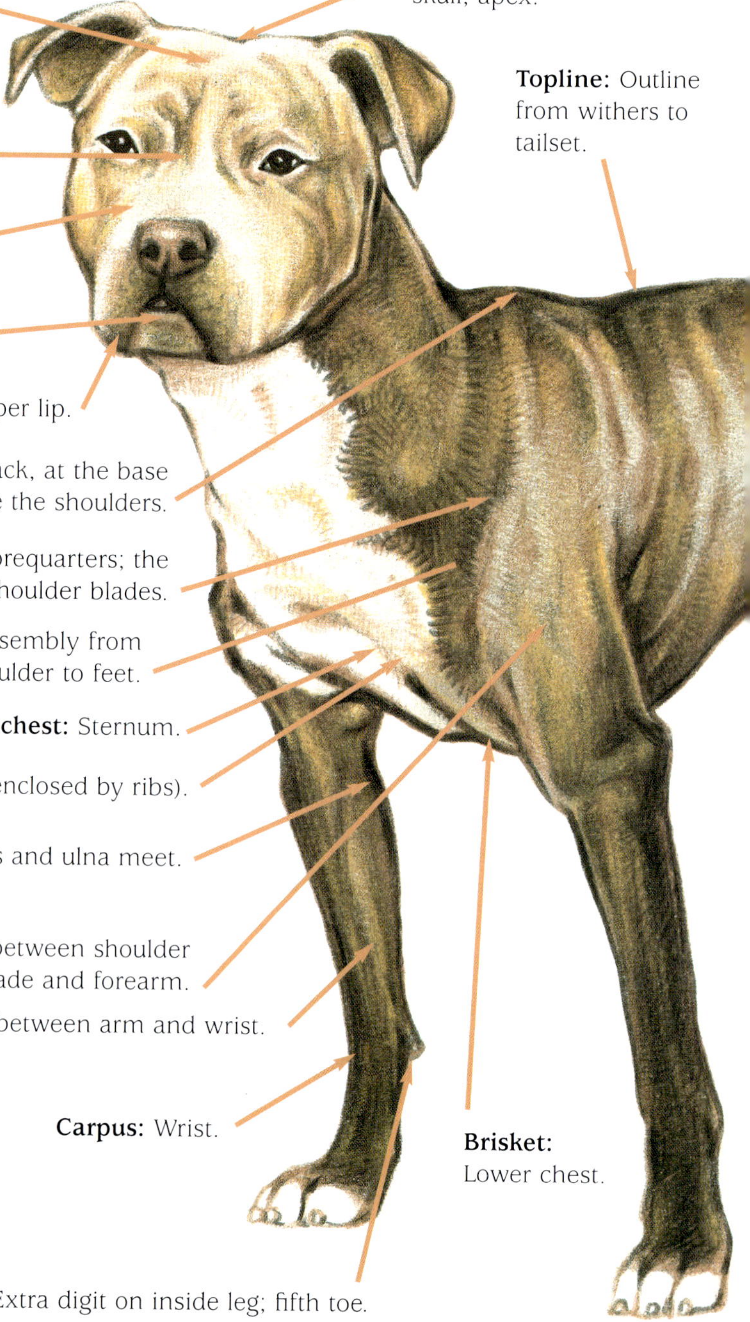

Skull: Cranium.

Stop: Indentation between the eyes at point of nasal bones and skull.

Muzzle: Foreface or region of head in front of eyes.

Lip: Fleshy portion of upper and lower jaws.

Flews: Hanging part of upper lip.

Withers: Highest part of the back, at the base of neck above the shoulders.

Shoulder: Upper point of forequarters; the region of the two shoulder blades.

Forequarters: Front assembly from shoulder to feet.

Forechest: Sternum.

Chest: Thoracic cavity (enclosed by ribs).

Elbow: Region where humerus and ulna meet.

Upper arm: Region between shoulder blade and forearm.

Forearm: Region between arm and wrist.

Carpus: Wrist.

Dewclaw: Extra digit on inside leg; fifth toe.

Occiput: Upper back part of skull; apex.

Topline: Outline from withers to tailset.

Brisket: Lower chest.

External Anatomy of the APBT*

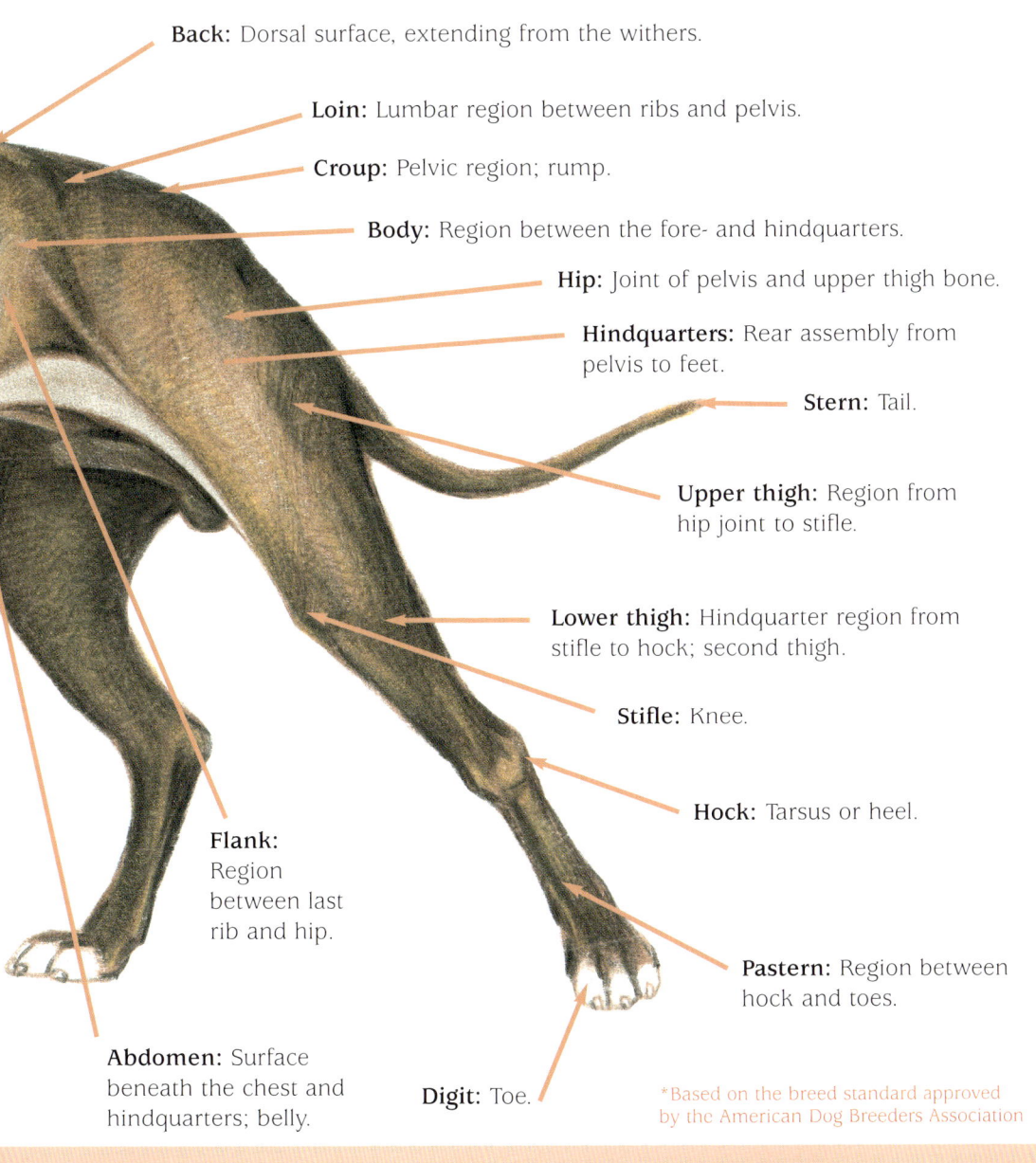

Back: Dorsal surface, extending from the withers.

Loin: Lumbar region between ribs and pelvis.

Croup: Pelvic region; rump.

Body: Region between the fore- and hindquarters.

Hip: Joint of pelvis and upper thigh bone.

Hindquarters: Rear assembly from pelvis to feet.

Stern: Tail.

Upper thigh: Region from hip joint to stifle.

Lower thigh: Hindquarter region from stifle to hock; second thigh.

Stifle: Knee.

Hock: Tarsus or heel.

Flank: Region between last rib and hip.

Pastern: Region between hock and toes.

Abdomen: Surface beneath the chest and hindquarters; belly.

Digit: Toe.

*Based on the breed standard approved by the American Dog Breeders Association

American Pit Bull Terrier

CHAPTER 2

you are looking for a guard dog, you are better off looking at the Belgian Malinois, Rottweiler or German Shepherd. If you like the looks of the APBT but do not feel qualified to do justice to this breed, you may want to consider an American Bulldog.

While considering the ABPT as a family pet, you will want to gather as much information on the breed as possible. Visit shows where the APBT is being exhibited so you can observe the breed, meet the handlers and benefit from their knowledge. Go to the library and check out other books on the APBT. In addition, there are several web sites where you can

The APBT can be considered a "head breed," as the impressive head is a most distinct and important feature of the dog.

Description of the APBT

access information. Good places to start are the American Dog Breeders Association (www.adba.cc) and the United Kennel Club (www.ukcdogs.com).

There is also an excellent periodical that you can subscribe to: *The American Pit Bull Terrier Gazette*, PO Box 1771, Salt Lake City, Utah 84110. This is also the address for the American Dog Breeders Association.

There are no restrictions regarding the APBT's color, markings or color patterns, which means that there's a wonderful rainbow available to prospective owners. This pair illustrates just two of the endless possibilities.

DESCRIPTION OF THE APBT

Overview

- The breed standard is an official description of the ideal APBT, detailing correct physical conformation as well as character and movement.
- The UKC and the ADBA each set forth a standard for the APBT. The UKC standard emphasizes the breed's strength; the ADBA standard reflects the breed's athleticism and traits that contributed to his original purpose. Although no longer a fighting dog, the APBT still should be built like one.
- The APBT is strong and muscular, seen in any color or pattern, with cropped or uncropped ears.
- People must see past the APBT's "bad rap" and get to know the wonderful qualities of this versatile, loyal and handsome companion.

CHAPTER 3

AMERICAN
PIT BULL TERRIER

Are You an APBT Person?

Before purchasing your APBT, you must give much thought to the personality and characteristics of the breed to determine if this is the right dog for you. This is not a dog for the laid-back owner who will not give the dog the training and attention that he deserves. In addition, this is not a dog for the first-time puppy owner. This is a dog for the individual who has studied up on the breed, understands its characteristics and is willing to train the dog and give him

APBTs are active dogs that require constructive outlets for their energy. The best type of exercise comes from activities done with their owners, which has the added benefit of strengthening their relationship.

the time that he will need.

You should consider the following issues before purchasing an APBT:

1. Do you have the time to give to a dog? He will need care, companionship, training and grooming. This is almost like having a child, except the dog remains a child and will always require your care.
2. Do you have a fenced-in yard for your Pit Bull? This is not a breed that you can tie out on the porch or let roam free. He must have a secure area in which to run and exercise.
3. Have you owned a dog previously and did that dog live a long and happy life with your family?
4. Have you checked with your town's offices to make certain that there are no breed-specific laws in your neighborhood? Some communities will not allow certain breeds of dog, and the APBT may be one of them.

A house with a fenced-in yard in which the dog can spend some time running and playing freely is an ideal living environment for the APBT.

The APBT is not a very tall dog; rather, he is compact and muscular, with more strength pound for pound than most other breeds.

CHAPTER 3

American Pit Bull Terrier

Every APBT has the potential to grow into a sweet and loving pet. Much depends on the owner, and how the dog is raised and trained.

Are You an APBT Person?

5. Understand that your neighbors may not be pleased with your bringing this dog into the neighborhood. Unfortunately, the Pit Bull is not looked upon kindly by many people who do not understand the breed or who have not had contact with a well-bred APBT.
6. Even if this breed requires a minimum of grooming, your dog will require some coat care. Do you have the time and interest to do this?

Let's look at each of these issues, one at a time:

1. Having time for a dog does not mean that you cannot work and own a dog. Your pet will need quality time, though, just as a child does. He must be fed two times a day and exercised several times a day. He needs to be petted and loved, and he will like to go for rides in the car with you. You must work with him and spend time with him to have an obedient dog who has good manners.

The APBT's short coat is easy to care for. Aside from brushing and occasional bathing, he will need his skin and coat checked regularly to make sure he hasn't picked up any insects or allergens outdoors.

Your dog should have at least two good outings a day, and that means a walk or a good romp in the morning and the evening. Never let him out loose to run the neighborhood. This is a breed that may not last long on the street because of the public's negative attitude. Many Pit Bulls are picked up by animal control and turned over to shelters every day.

American Pit Bull Terrier

2. Do you have a fenced-in yard? This should give you at least enough space to throw a ball and for your dog to run with it. Remember, it is your responsibility to keep the yard clean of dog feces. When walking your dog, it is essential to carry a plastic bag or two to pick up droppings. These can be easily dropped in a handy trash receptacle on your way home.

3. Have you owned a dog previously? This will give you a good idea of what a dog expects from you and what you must do for your dog. Since the APBT is one of the strongest dogs in the canine world, you must be able to handle him. In addition, like other terriers, the Pit Bull is smart and needs an owner that is smarter than he is!

4. Be sure to check with your town or city and find out if

The APBT is an impressive-looking dog, handsome and dignified with a range of striking colors and markings, like this dog's white blaze.

Are You an APBT Person?

Breeders' Best

This picture tells volumes about the APBT's ever-alert nature.

American Pit Bull Terrier

there are any anti-Pit-Bull or other breed-specific laws for your area. If your local council has banned certain breeds in the area, you can be almost certain that this ban will include the Pit Bull.

5. You should talk to your neighbors about adding an APBT to your household. Give them some information on the breed and reassure them that you are purchasing a sound, well-bred puppy from a responsible breeder.

6. Grooming is minimal with this breed, but you will need to go over him with a brush, trim his toenails, wash his face once or twice a week, keep his ears clean and give him a bath as needed.

Anyone considering APBT ownership must enjoy keeping active and be willing to spend time participating in activities with his dog. It doesn't have to be all structured; the APBT is a playful animal that will enjoy just goofing off with his owner. That being said, in order to fully enjoy activities together, the dog must be well trained and well behaved. The owner must make a commitment to his dog's training so that his APBT is a mannerly and reliable dog around everyone. You cannot take a chance with such a strong breed; added to that is the

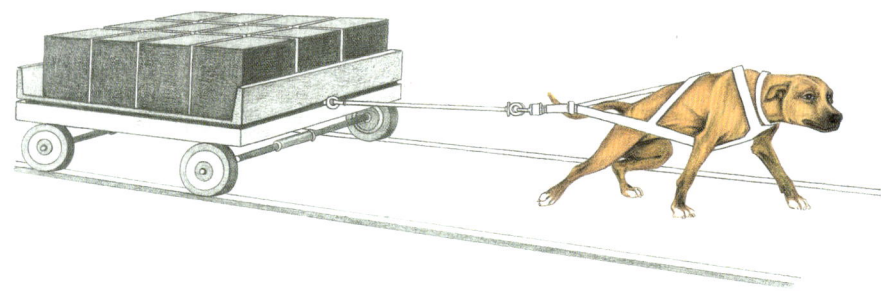

Breed aficionados often like to train their dogs for weight-pulling competitions and are amazed by their dogs' strength and tenacity.

Are You an APBT Person?

Breeders' Best

public's generally negative view of the "Pit Bull." If your APBT is a good canine citizen, not only will you have a wonderful relationship with him but you also will be presenting the breed in a positive light.

APBTs can be dog-aggressive, but it is possible to keep them successfully in multi-dog households. There are no problems here!

ARE YOU AN APBT PERSON?
Overview

- The APBT person has carefully considered all of the pros and cons of APBT ownership and is sure that he can raise his dog to be a model canine citizen.
- The APBT person has time to exercise, care for and train his dog, and can provide ample accommodations.
- The APBT person is a responsible dog owner and wants an APBT for the right reasons—*not* for protection, aggression or fighting. He will train his dog reliably and promote the positive qualities of the breed.
- The APBT person makes certain that his dog is safe at all times.

CHAPTER 4

AMERICAN PIT BULL TERRIER

Selecting an APBT Breeder

When you buy your APBT, you will want to buy a sound, healthy puppy from a responsible breeder. A responsible breeder is someone who has given considerable thought before breeding his bitch. He considers health problems in the breed, has room in his home or kennel for a litter of puppies and has the time to give to a litter. He does not breed to the dog down the block because it is easy and because

What a handsome pair! All puppies in the litter from which you choose your pup should be healthy, alert, friendly and otherwise sound.

he wants to show his children the miracle of birth. A reputable breeder, whose kennel or line has been nationally known for five or ten generations, does not breed Pit Bulls for profit. He knows that breeding dogs is a labor of love. The cost of raising a litter and maintaining a kennel are prohibitive: this is a business that is usually in the red (the color of "love").

Part of the excitement of visiting the breeder is meeting the litter. This gives you a chance to have some fun while getting to know each pup's personality and finding one best suited to you.

A responsible breeder is someone who is dedicated to the breed and committed to breeding out any faults and hereditary problems, and whose overall interest is in improving the breed. He will study pedigrees and see what the leading stud dogs are producing. To find the right stud dog for his bitch, he may fly his bitch across the country to breed to a particular stud dog, or he may drive the bitch to the dog, often traveling hundreds of miles away. The breeder may produce only one or two litters a

Father and pup. The puppy has inherited the striking brindle pattern.

American Pit Bull Terrier

year, which means that there may not be a puppy ready for you when you first call. Remember that you are purchasing a new family member, so waiting for the right puppy will be well worthwhile.

The responsible Pit Bull breeder will probably be someone who has been breeding for some years, someone who is known on the national level. Check out the *American Pit Bull Terrier Gazette* or talk to someone at the American Dog Breeders Association for leads in finding a responsible breeder.

The responsible breeder will show you his kennel, if he has a kennel, or will invite you into his home to see the puppies. The areas will be clean and smell good. The breeder will show you the dam of the puppy that you are looking at and she will look and smell clean, and will be groomed.

When meeting the litter, don't be afraid to get down on the puppies' level.

Selecting an APBT Breeder

The puppies will also be clean, with trimmed toenails and clean faces. The breeder will show you the puppies, but likely he will not show you those that are already sold or that he is going to keep.

The breeder will also have questions for you. Have you had a dog before? How many have you had? Have you ever owned an APBT? Did your dogs live long lives? Do you have a fenced yard? How many children do you have and what are their ages? Have you ever done any dog training? Are there any other pets in your household? Do not be offended by these questions. He has put much effort and money into his litter and his first priority is to place each pup in a caring and appropriate household where the pup will be wanted, loved and cared for properly.

Sometimes your puppy will march right up and pick you!

SELECTING AN APBT BREEDER

Overview

- Contact reputable clubs, like the American Dog Breeders Association, to help you find an ethical breeder.
- When visiting the breeder, take a look around and meet all of his dogs and puppies. Be sure you are satisfied with the condition of the dogs and their living quarters.
- Expect to be interviewed by the breeder and answer him honestly; this will help the breeder find your perfect puppy match and assure him that you will be a fit owner.

AMERICAN
PIT BULL TERRIER

Finding the Right APBT Puppy

You are now ready to select your puppy. You have decided that you are an APBT person and that you can live with this determined, courageous and smart dog. You have checked out the local ordinances for breed-specific legislation and you have talked to your neighbors about bringing a Pit Bull into the community. Your entire family is ready for this new arrival into your home and lives. You have done your homework and have located a reputable breeder who

For the first weeks of life, Mom is the teacher, instructing her pups in the ways of the canine world.

has a litter available.

You arrive at the appointed time and the breeder has the puppies ready for you to look at. They should be a happy bunch, clean and groomed. Their noses will be wet, their coats will have a glow or sheen and they will have a nice covering of flesh over their ribs. You will be ready to pick up one of these rascals and cuddle him in your arms.

You should ask the breeder if the sire and dam of the litter have had their temperaments tested. These tests are offered by the American Temperament Test Society (ATTS) and responsible breeders of Pit Bulls will be familiar with this organization and will have had their animals tested. The breeder will show you the score sheets and you can easily determine if the litter's parents have the personalities you are looking for. In addition, this is an excellent indication that this is a responsible breeder.

When meeting puppies from the litter, engage them in play to see their personalities come to life.

Puppies nurse until about the sixth week and should be fully weaned by around the eighth week, when it's time for them to go to their new homes.

CHAPTER 5
American Pit Bull Terrier

Breeders who raise their pups in the home, allowing them to be part of family life rather than isolating them in kennels, are doing new owners a big favor in socializing the pups and getting them ready to make the transition to their human packs. It's a big advantage for the pups, too.

Finding the Right APBT Puppy

Breeders' Best

Temperament testing by the ATTS is done on dogs that are at least 18 months of age; therefore puppies are not tested, but the sire and dam of a litter can be tested. The test is like a simulated walk through a park or a neighborhood where everyday situations are encountered. Neutral, friendly and threatening situations are encountered to see what the dog's reactions are to the various stimuli. Problems that are looked for are unprovoked aggression, panic without recovery and strong avoidance. The dog is observed for behavior toward strangers, reaction to auditory, visual and tactile stimuli and self-protective and aggressive behavior. The dog is on a loose lead for the test, which takes about ten minutes to complete. As of December 2002, 405 APBTs had taken the test, with 337 passing, for a percentage rate of 83.2%,

Always insist on meeting the dam and, if he is on the premises, the sire of the litter. You want to make sure that your pup comes from temperamentally sound and healthy stock.

which places the breed in one of the upper percentiles for good temperament.

Some breeders will have the temperaments of their puppies tested by either a professional, their veterinarian or another dog breeder. They will find the high-energy pup and the pup that is slower to respond. They will find the pup with the independent spirit and the one that will want to follow the pack. If the litter has been tested, the breeder will suggest which pup he thinks will be best for your family. Even without formal testing, the breeder will know

The whelping box is lined with soft, absorbent material, as it initially functions as the pups' bedroom, living room, bathroom, playroom, etc.

Finding the Right APBT Puppy

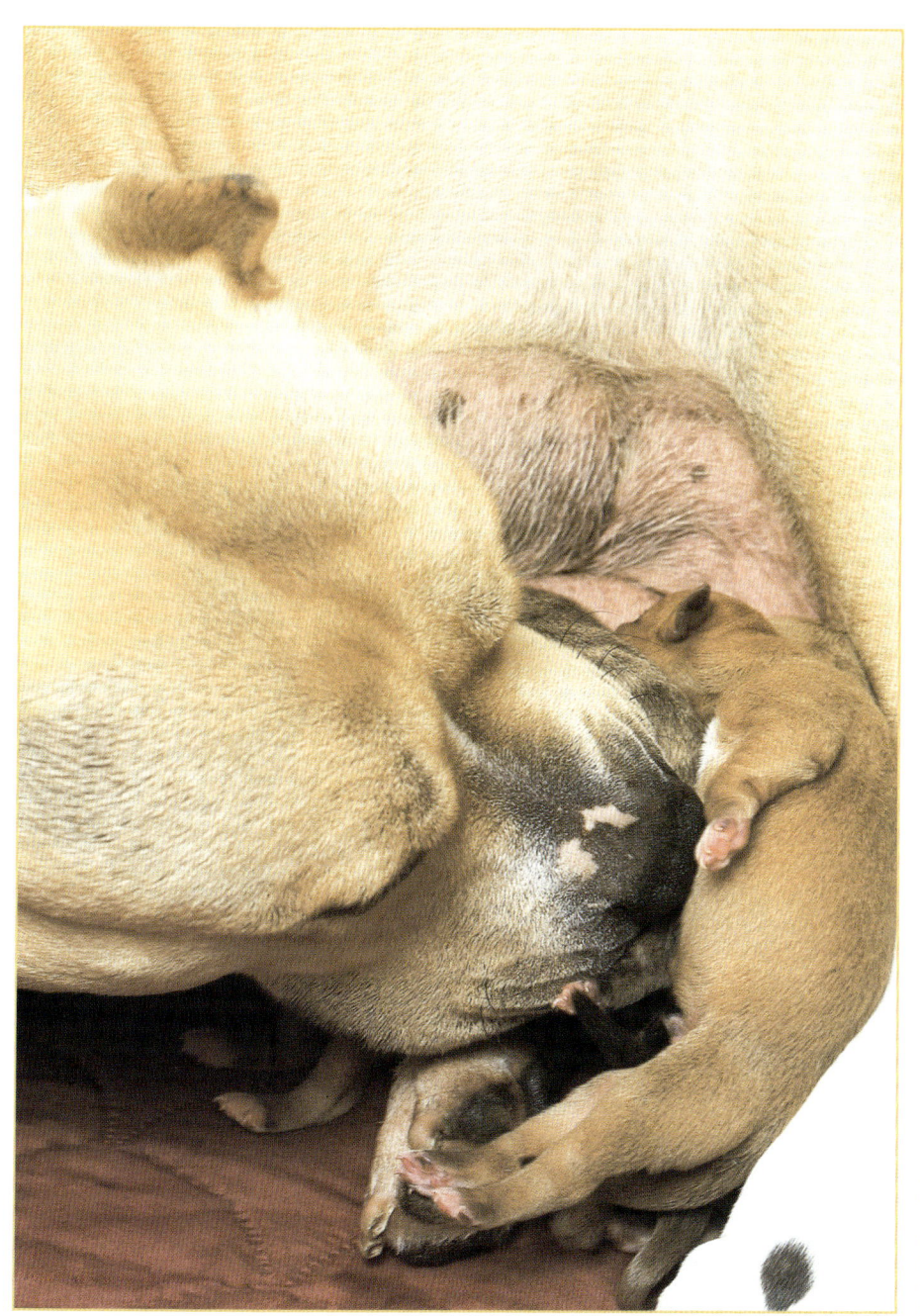

Breeders' Best

APBT females make attentive moms who lovingly nurture their babies.

CHAPTER 5

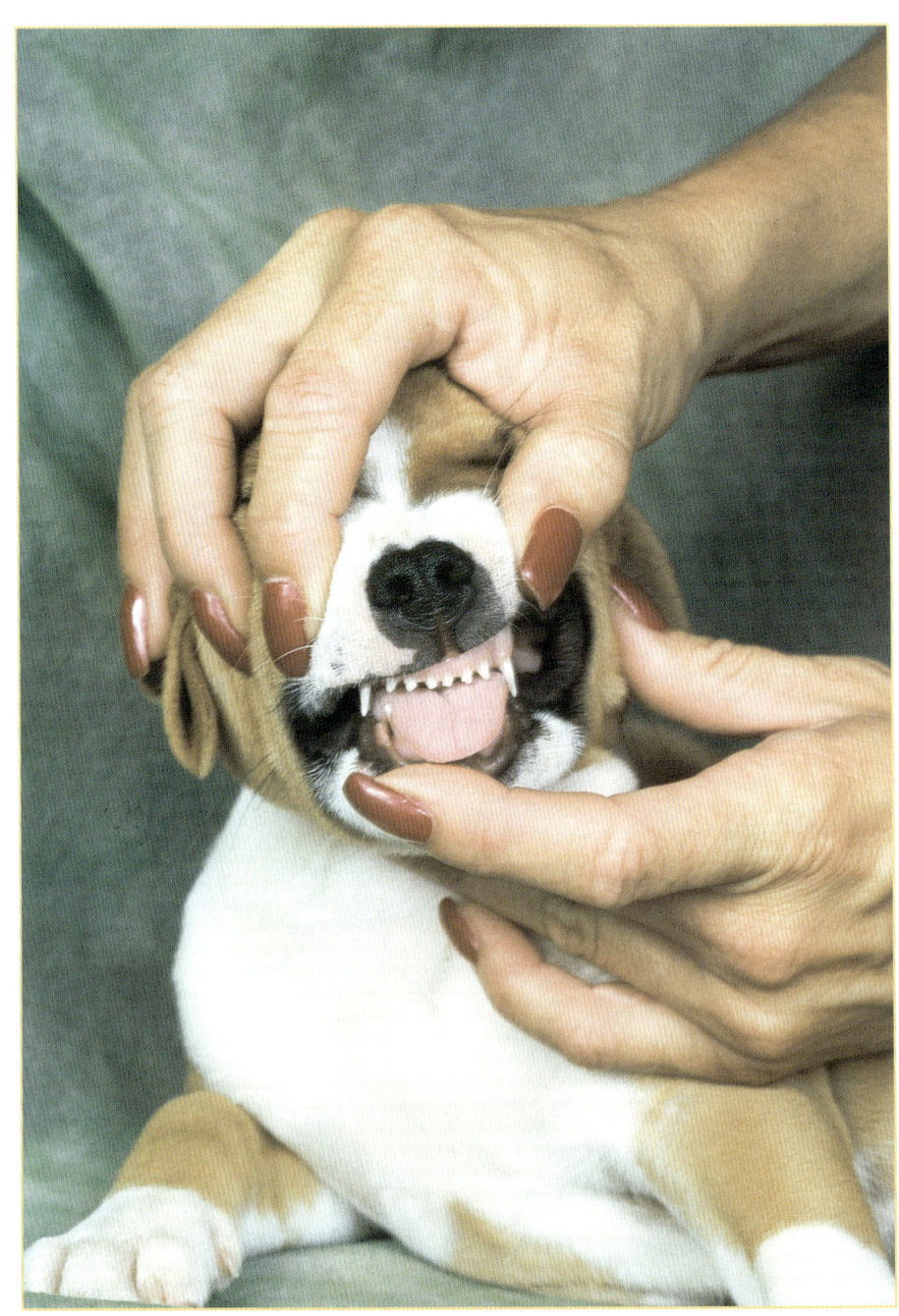

American Pit Bull Terrier

Check the bite of your chosen puppy. The jaw is an important characteristic of the APBT, so you want a pup with well-placed teeth and a correctly formed mouth.

Finding the Right APBT Puppy

Breeders' Best

each pup very well.

If the litter has not been tested, you can do a few simple tests while you are sitting on the floor, playing with the pups. Pat your leg or snap your finger and see which pup comes up to you first. Clap your hands and see if one of the litter shies away from you. See how they play with one another. Watch for the one that has the personality most appealing to you, as this will probably be the puppy that you take home. Look for the puppy that appears to be "in the middle," not overly rambunctious, overly aggressive or submissive. You want the joyful pup, not the wild one.

Spend some time selecting your puppy. If you are hesitant, tell the breeder that you would like to go home and think over your decision. This is a major addition to the family, as this dog may be with you for 10 to 15 years. Be sure you get the puppy that you will all be happy with. You are now on your way to bringing your new puppy into your household!

FINDING THE RIGHT APBT PUPPY

Overview

- Visit the litter to see the puppies and observe them in action. You are seeking healthy, sound puppies. They should be much more than "cute": bright eyes, shiny coats and stable personalities count for a lot.
- Trust the breeder whom you've selected to recommend a puppy that fits your lifestyle and personality.
- Ask the breeder about temperament testing and health clearances on the litter's parents, and ask to see relevant documentation.
- Make your decision carefully and get ready for your new family member!

CHAPTER 6

AMERICAN
PIT BULL TERRIER

Welcoming the APBT

You have selected your puppy and are ready to bring your new family member home. Before welcoming your pup, you should buy food and water bowls, a leash and a collar. You should also purchase a crate for your puppy not only to sleep in but also to spend his time in when he is home alone. In very short order, your puppy will learn that the crate is his "second home." He will feel safe and secure when he is in his crate. When the pup is left uncrated

Sometimes breeders will acclimate their pups to crates for short periods of time, making the crate-training process easier for new owners. Once in their new homes, though, it's only one pup per crate!

and alone, he will quickly become bored and begin to chew on the furniture, the corners of woodwork, etc. Keeping him in a confined area (his crate) when you are away will eliminate his getting into mischief or danger. Be sure to put several towels or a washable blanket in the crate so that he will be comfortable.

If you are driving some distance to pick up your pet, take along a towel or two, a water bowl, his leash and his collar. Also take along some plastic baggies and a roll of paper towels in case there are any potty accidents on the way home.

Before bringing your puppy into the house, you should be aware that a small puppy can be like a toddler and that there are dangers in the household that must be removed. Electrical wires should be raised off the floor and hidden from view, as they are very tempting as chewable objects. Swimming pools can be very

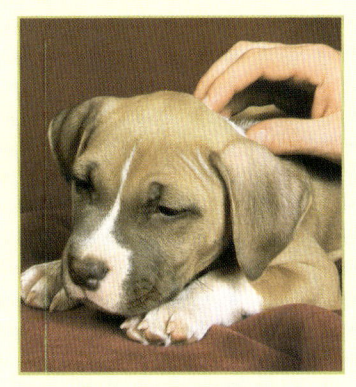

Gentle petting and attention, without overwhelming the pup, will help him ease into life with his new family in his new home.

Give your pup time to explore his new surroundings, indoors and out, under your watchful eye, of course.

American Pit Bull Terrier

dangerous, so make certain that your puppy can't get into, or fall into, the pool. Some barricades will be necessary to prevent an accident. Not all dogs can swim, and those with short legs or heavy bodies cannot climb out of the pool. Watch your deck railings and make sure that your puppy cannot slip through the openings. Household chemicals can be dangerous; some, like antifreeze, can kill a dog quickly in just a small amount. Keep all cleaning products and other chemicals locked away in areas to which the pup does not have access.

If you have young children in the house, you must be sure that they understand that the small puppy is a living being and must be treated gently. They cannot ride on him or pull his ears, and he cannot be picked up and dropped. This is your responsibility. A child taught about animals at an early age can become a lifelong compassionate animal lover and owner.

Soft toys will be much appreciated by your teething APBT, but keep in mind that a stuffed toy can be destroyed by puppy teeth in no time! Once past the teething stage, he will require indestructible chew toys designed for the strongest dogs.

Welcoming the APBT

Breeders' Best

Flat buckle collar, which can be made of leather or woven nylon.

Adjustable nylon quick-release collars come in many colors and patterns and work well for growing puppies.

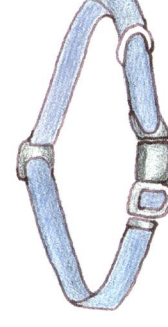

Rolled leather collar with brass hardware.

Martingale, or humane chain-choke collar, which also comes in nylon.

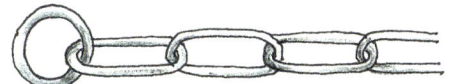

Fur-saver, large-link choke collar.

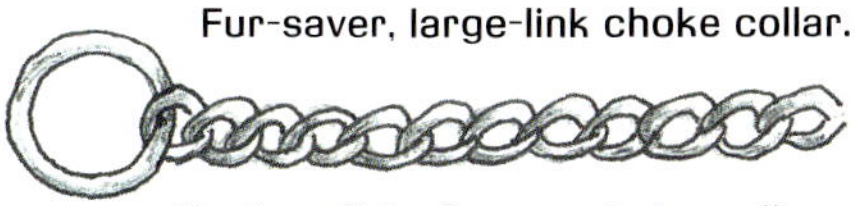

Medium-link chrome choke collar.

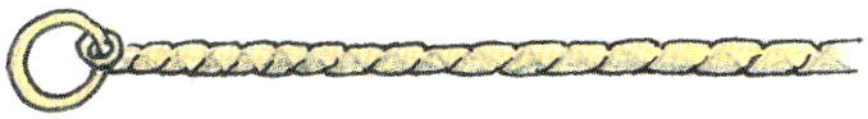

Brass snake-chain protects coat and is often used in the show ring.

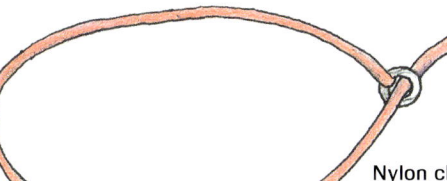

Nylon choke collar, which comes in many colors and thicknesses.

Drawing by Patricia Peters

American Pit Bull Terrier

Use your common sense in all safety issues concerning the puppy. Consider where a young child can get into trouble, and your puppy will be right behind him!

When the pup comes into the house for the first time (after he has relieved himself outside), let him look at his new home and surroundings. Give him a light meal and a bowl of water. When he is tired, take him outside to relieve himself again and then tuck him into his crate, either to take a nap or, hopefully, to sleep through the night.

The first day or two for your puppy should be fairly quiet. He will then have time to get used to his new home, surroundings and family members. The first night, he may cry a bit, but if you put a teddy bear or a soft, woolly sweater in his crate, it will give him some warmth and security. A nearby ticking clock or a radio playing soft music can also be helpful. Remember, he has been uprooted from his siblings, his mother and his familiar breeder, and he will need a day or two to get used to his new family. If he should cry during the first night, let him be and he will eventually quiet down and sleep. By the third night, he should be well settled in. Have patience and, within a week or less, it will seem to you, your family and the puppy that you have all been together for years.

Nutrition for your puppy is

A few treats, and your new APBT will feel at home in no time!

Welcoming the APBT

actually very easy. Dog-food companies hire many scientists and spend millions of dollars on research to determine what will be a healthy diet for your dog. Your breeder should have been feeding a premium puppy food, and you should continue on with the same brand. The author recommends top-quality dog foods preferably manufactured by small companies that can afford to invest in human-quality ingredients with a minimum of 23% protein. These foods will have chicken, lamb or turkey meal as their primary ingredients, be labeled "best-used-by" a certain date and indicate that the product meets the AAFCO's standard for nutrition. As the dog matures, you will change over to the adult brand of the same dog food. Do not add vitamins or anything else unless your veterinarian suggests that you do so. Do not think that, by cooking up a special diet, you will turn out a product that will be more nutritional than what the dog-food companies are providing.

Your young puppy will probably be fed three times a day and perhaps as many as four times a day. As he starts growing, you will cut his meals to two times a day, in the morning and in the evening. By the time he reaches eight months of age, you will be changing over to the adult dog food. You can

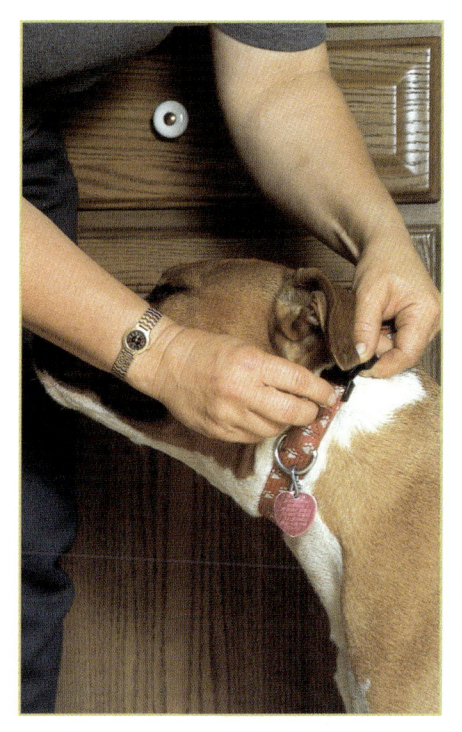

Your APBT's collar, with his ID tag attached securely, should be worn at all times.

CHAPTER 6

American Pit Bull Terrier

The lead that you use for a grown APBT will be much stronger than that used for a puppy. For extra-strong dogs like the APBT, many owners prefer to use thick nylon harnesses for routine walks.

Welcoming the APBT

check the dog-food container for the amount, per pound of weight, that you should be feeding your dog. You may add water to moisten the dry food and possibly add a tablespoon or so of a canned dog food for flavor. Avoid giving table scraps, and give him a dog treat at bedtime. Keep a good covering of flesh over his ribs, but do not let your APBT become a fat boy! However, the more active the dog, the more calories he will need. Always have fresh drinking water available. This may include a bowl of water in the kitchen and another outside in the yard for when he is outdoors.

You are now off to an excellent start with your puppy. As the days go by, you will quickly find more items that you will need, including some tough chew toys and a retractable leash for walks in the park. You will need grooming supplies and a good pooper scooper for cleaning up the yard. These items can be acquired as needed from your local pet shop.

WELCOMING THE APBT
Overview

- Be prepared with the basics before bringing the pup home. Among the items you'll need are food, bowls, a collar and ID tags, toys, a leash, a crate, a brush and a comb.
- Make your home safe for your puppy by removing hazards from the dog's environment indoors and out.
- Introduce the pup to any children in the home carefully and supervise their interactions.
- Allow your pup a few days' time to settle in.
- Take advice from the breeder about a proper diet and changes to be made as the pup matures.

CHAPTER 7

AMERICAN PIT BULL TERRIER

House-training and More

Your dog must be housebroken. This job should begin as soon as you bring him home. Diligence during the first two or three weeks will surely pay off. House-breaking your APBT pup should be a relatively easy task since the breed is so smart.

Every time your puppy wakes up from a nap, he should be quickly taken outside. Watch him and praise him with "Good boy!" when he urinates or defecates. Give him a pat on the head and take him inside. He may have a

Learn to recognize the signs! An intense look on your pup's face and a half-squatting posture means that he has to "go" now!

48

Breeders' Best

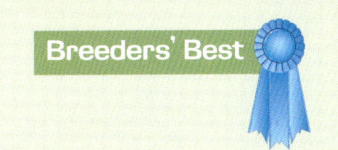

few accidents but, with the appropriate "No" from you, he will quickly learn that it is better to go outside and do his "business" than to do it on the kitchen floor and be scolded.

You will soon learn your dog's habits. However, at the following times it is essential to take your dog out: when he gets up in the morning, after he eats, before he goes to bed and after long naps. As dogs mature, most will have to go out only three or four times a day. Some dogs will go to the door and bark when they want to be let out and others will nervously circle around. Watch and learn from your pup's signs. Of course, crates are a major help in housebreaking, as most dogs will not want to dirty their living quarters.

Just be patient with housebreaking, as this can sometimes be a trying time. It is simply essential to have a clean house dog. Life will be much easier for all of you—not to

Your puppy will learn to go to his chosen relief spot on his own quite quickly.

For owners without a fenced yard, taking the dog out on his lead for bathroom breaks will be necessary; remember to always clean up after him.

CHAPTER 7

American Pit Bull Terrier

mention better for the carpeting!

NAME RECOGNITION
Puppy must learn to respond to his name (name recognition), and you must be able to gain and hold his attention. You can accomplish this with positive association of the puppy's name: "Good, Gustav" as well as with treats. Treats are defined as small tidbits, preferably soft easy-to-chew treats. We don't want to overfeed this pup. Thin slices of hotdogs cut into quarters work well, as do small pieces of cheese or cooked chicken.

Start by calling your Pit Bull puppy's name. Once. Not two or three times, but once. Otherwise, he will learn he has a multi-part name and will ignore you when you say it once. Begin by using his name when he is undistracted and you know that he will look at you, and pop him a treat as soon as he looks at you. Repeat at least a dozen times, several times a day. It won't take more than a day or so before he understands that his name means something good to eat.

TIMING
All dogs learn their lessons in the present tense. You have to catch them in the act

If you have a fenced yard, train your pup to relieve himself in the same area each time. Start out by leading him there on his leash whenever you take him out for potty time.

House-training and More

Breeders' Best

(good or bad) in order to dispense rewards or discipline. You have five seconds to connect with your dog or he will not understand what he did wrong. Thus, timing and consistency are your keys to success in teaching any new behavior or correcting bad behaviors.

Keep in mind while training: use your common sense, be consistent and have patience. Just when you may think that all is hopeless, your puppy turns into the perfect little gentleman.

House-training is the key to a happy and clean life for all parties, human and canine!

HOUSE-TRAINING YOUR APBT

Overview

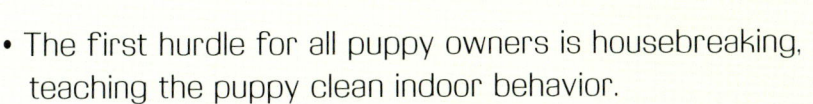

- The first hurdle for all puppy owners is housebreaking, teaching the puppy clean indoor behavior.
- Know when your puppy needs to go outside and always praise him when he "goes" where he should.
- Train your puppy to respond to his name and pay attention to you.
- Teach your puppy good manners for the car and keep his safety foremost in your mind when traveling.
- Know that in order to connect with the dog you must catch him in the act, whether for rewards or discipline.

CHAPTER 8

AMERICAN
PIT BULL TERRIER

Your APBT's Education

Your puppy should be well socialized when you bring him home. He will be used to family and strangers. Average noises in the house and on the street will not startle him. Socialization for your puppy is very important, and good breeders will begin socialization early on. It's particularly good if there are children in the breeder's family, as the puppy will have become used to youngsters.

Once he is adjusted to his new home, let your pup meet the neighbors and play for a few minutes. Take him for short walks in public places where he will see people and

Spending time with his mother is part of the pup's early socialization and the first type of education he receives.

Breeders' Best

other dogs as well as hear strange noises. Watch other dogs, however, as they are not always friendly. Keep your dog on a short leash and you will have control over him so he does not jump up on anyone or any other dog.

You must have a well-behaved and mannerly dog; therefore there are some basic commands that you and your dog must understand to make your dog a better citizen. One of the family members should attend Puppy Kindergarten classes, from which all other training and activities will grow. This is a class that accepts puppies from two to five months of age. It will take about two months to complete the class. You will cover the basics: sit, heel, down and recall (or come). There are definite advantages to each. Sit and heel are great helps when walking your dog. Who needs a puppy walking between your legs, lunging forward or lagging behind, in general acting like a nut? Have your dog walking like a

With a breed like the APBT, socialization that starts early and continues through adulthood cannot be emphasized enough. You want your dog to be well behaved and amenable to meeting other people and canines.

You'll find the greatest success in training if you start when the pup is young, with nothing on his mind other than showing you how much he loves you and wants to please you.

American Pit Bull Terrier

gentleman on your left side and sitting as you wait to cross the street. The recall (come) is very important if your dog either escapes from the yard or breaks his leash. You will need to call him back and know that he will return to you reliably.

Here is a short rundown of the commands. If you attend puppy classes or obedience-training classes, you will have professional help in learning these commands. However, you and your dog can learn these very basic exercises on your own.

SIT COMMAND
This is the first exercise you should teach. Place your dog on your left side as you are standing and say firmly "Sit." As you say this, run your hand down your dog's back and gently push him into a sitting position. Praise him and hold him in this position for a few minutes, then release your hand, praise him again and give him a treat. Repeat this several times a day, perhaps as many as ten times, throughout the day. Before long, your pup will understand what you want.

COME COMMAND
This command has life-saving potential… preventing your American Pit Bull Terrier from running into the street, going after a squirrel, chasing a child on a bike, the list goes on and on.

Always practice this command on leash. You can't afford to risk failure, or your pup will learn that he does not have to come when called. Once you have the pup's attention, call him from a short distance with "Puppy, come!" (use your happy voice!) and give a treat when he comes to you. If

Your APBT's Education

he hesitates, tug him to you gently with his leash. Grasp and hold his collar with one hand as you dispense the treat. This is important. You will eventually phase out the treat and switch to hands-on praise. This maneuver also connects holding his collar with coming and treating, which will assist you in countless future behaviors. Do 10 or 12 repetitions 2 or 3 times a day. Once the pup has mastered the come command, continue to practice daily to engrave this most important behavior into his puppy brain. Experienced APBT owners know, however, that you can never completely trust a dog to come when called if the dog is bent on a self-appointed mission. "Off-leash" is often synonymous with "out of control."

As you tell your dog to "sit," use one hand to give him a gentle push on the rump to guide him into the sitting position while you hold the lead with your other hand.

STAY COMMAND

Teach your dog to stay in a seated position until you call him. Have your dog sit and, as you say "Stay,"

American Pit Bull Terrier

place your hand in front of his nose and take a step or two, no more at the beginning, away from him. After ten seconds or so, call your dog. If he gets up before the end of the command, have him sit again and repeat the stay command. When he stays until called (remembering to start with a very short period of time), praise him and give him a treat. As he learns this command, increase the space that you move away from the dog as well as the length of time that he stays.

Training is a one-on-one exercise. Too many cooks can spoil the soup and confuse the dog.

HEEL COMMAND

Have your dog on your left side, with his leash on, and teach him to walk with you. If your pup lunges forward, give the leash a quick snap and say a firm "No." Then continue to walk your dog, praising him as he walks nicely by your side. Again, if he lunges, snap his leash quickly and say a smart "No." He will quickly learn that it is easier and more pleasant to walk by your side. Never allow him to lunge at someone passing by you.

DOWN COMMAND

This will probably be the most complicated of the five basic commands to teach. Place your dog in the sit position, kneel down next to him and place your right hand under his front legs and your left hand on his shoulders. As you say "Down," gently push his front legs out into the down

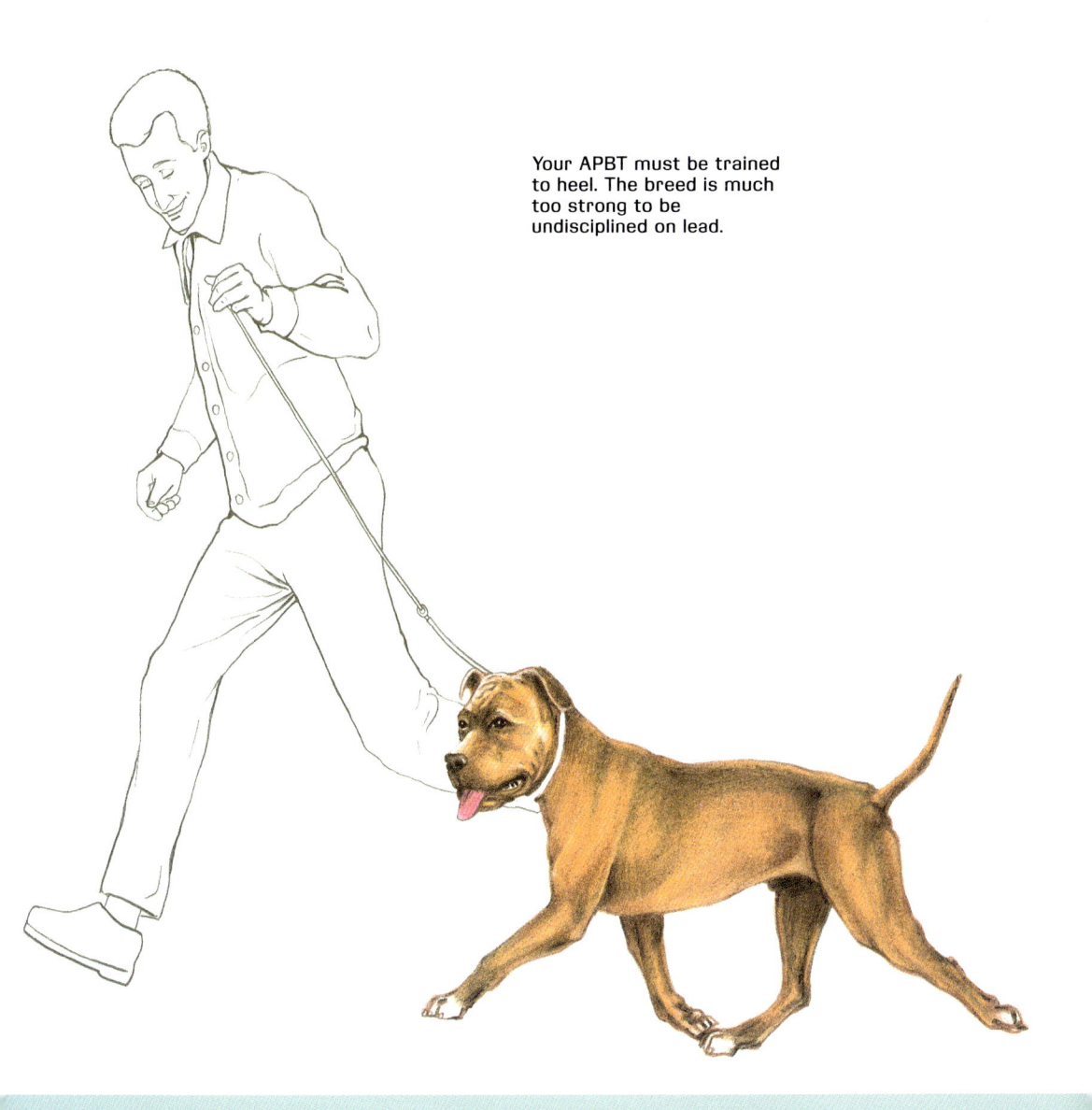

Your APBT's Education

Breeders' Best

Your APBT must be trained to heel. The breed is much too strong to be undisciplined on lead.

CHAPTER 8

American Pit Bull Terrier

The down position indicates submission and thus is never a dog's favorite exercise. Once you've accomplished the down, you can begin teaching the down/stay.

Your APBT's Education

position. You may want to move a treat away from him on the ground so that he follows the treat and thus assumes the down position. Once you have him down, talk gently to him, stroke his back so that he will be comfortable and then praise and treat him.

Big parts of training are patience, persistence and routine. Teach each command the same way every time, using the same verbal command. Do not lose your patience with the dog, as he will not understand what you are doing. Reward him—always with praise and sometimes a treat—for doing his command properly. With an APBT, you will find that your puppy will learn these commands very quickly. While bearing in mind how intelligent and trainable the APBT is, responsible first-time owners should consider hiring a professional dog trainer who has experience with the breed. It is better to invest in the services of a professional than to live with a dog who behaves poorly and doesn't heed your commands.

YOUR APBT'S EDUCATION

Overview

- The basis of training begins with socialization to other people, dogs and situations outside the family and home.
- Consider Puppy Kindergarten to get started with training in an environment with other people and puppies and a professional trainer.
- The basic commands include sit, come (recall), stay, heel and down.
- Use praise and treats in training. Use positive reinforcement to motivate your APBT to perform commands reliably.
- Keep practicing! Your APBT is a quick learner and you'll be thrilled with your polite, well-behaved canine companion.

CHAPTER 9

AMERICAN PIT BULL TERRIER

Home Care for Your APBT

Every home with a pet should have a first-aid kit. You can acquire all of these items at one time to have on hand or you can add them to your kit (keep your items together in a box) as you need them. Here are the items you will need:

• Alcohol for cleaning a wound;
• Antibiotic salve for treating the wound;
• Over-the-counter eye wash in case your dog gets something in his eyes or just needs to have his eyes cleaned—"to get the red out";

Who knows what pests lurk in the tall grass? Be diligent in checking your APBT's skin and coat for any abnormalities.

Breeders' Best

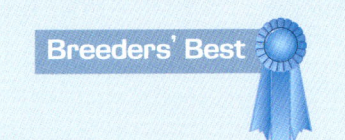

- Forceps for pulling out wood ticks, thorns and burs;
- Styptic powder for when a toenail has been trimmed too short and bleeds;
- Rectal thermometer;
- A nylon stocking to be used as a muzzle if your pet should be badly injured.

Many of these items can be purchased very reasonably from your local drug store; you may even have some of them already. Become educated about canine first aid so you can recognize signs of an emergency and take action right away while awaiting veterinary advice.

When your dog is mature and remaining well, he will only need a yearly visit to the veterinary clinic for a checkup and a booster shot for his vaccines. At these visits, the vet should always give a thorough dental evaluation and may express your dog's anal glands.

Daily time spent with your Pit Bull helps you to know your dog's habits, likes and dislikes. When he's feeling "off," you will know it immediately.

Begin inspecting your APBT's mouth while he's a puppy; eventually he will learn to tolerate this type of handling.

You may purchase a dental tool and clean the teeth yourself between veterinary visits. Set the dog on your grooming table and gently scrape away any tartar. Some dogs will let you do this and others will not. An easier option is regular tooth-brushing with a specially made canine toothpaste and toothbrush. A dog treat every night before bedtime will also help to keep the tartar down.

Expressing the anal glands is not the most enjoyable task, besides being quite smelly. You may find that it is easier to have this done during the yearly trip to the vet's clinic. On occasion, the anal glands will become impacted. This will require veterinary assistance to clean out the glands.

By now, you know your dog well, you know how much he eats and sleeps and how hard he plays. As with all of us, on occasion he may "go off" his food or appear to be sick. If he has been nauseated for 24 to 36 hours, had diarrhea for the same amount of time or has been drinking excessive water for five or six days, a trip to the veterinarian is in order. Make your appointment and tell the receptionist why you need the appointment right away.

The veterinarian will ask you the following questions:
- When did he last eat a normal meal?
- How long has he had diarrhea or been vomiting?
- Has he eaten anything in the last 24 hours?
- Could he have eaten a toy, a piece of clothing or anything else unusual?
- Is he drinking more water than usual?

The veterinarian will check him over, take his temperature and pulse, listen to his heart, feel his stomach for any lumps, look at his gums and teeth for color and check his eyes and ears. He

Home Care for Your APBT

Breeders' Best

In hot weather, dogs can succumb to heatstroke quickly. He should have access to plenty of shade outdoors, and a damp towel will help cool him off when it's hot outdoors.

will probably also draw blood to run tests.

At the end of the examination, the vet likely will either send your dog home with you with some antibiotics, take some x-rays or keep the dog overnight for observation. Follow your veterinarian's instructions and you will find that very often your dog will be back to normal in a day or two. In the meantime, feed him light meals and keep him quiet, perhaps confined to his crate.

Parasites can be a problem and there are certain ones of which you should be aware. Heartworm can be a deadly problem and some parts of the country can be more prone to this than others. Heartworms become very massive and wrap themselves around the dog's heart. If not treated, the dog will eventually die. Ask your vet if your dog should have a heartworm test. If so, take him to the clinic and he will be given a test to make certain that he is clear of heartworm, and then he will be put on heartworm preventative medication. This is important, particularly if you live where mosquitoes are present, as heartworms are transmitted by mosquitoes.

Fleas are also a problem,

Hands-on examinations are the only way to detect problems that are not apparent to the eye. Regular petting and hugging can turn up small lumps, bumps, etc., that may be present under the coat.

Home Care for Your APBT

but particularly in the warmer parts of the country. You can purchase flea powder or a collar from the pet shop or ask your veterinarian what he suggests that you use. If you suspect fleas, lay your dog on his side, separate the coat to the skin and look for any skipping, jumping or skittering around of little bugs.

Ticks are more prevalent in areas where there are numerous trees. Ticks are small (to start) and dark, and they like to attach themselves to the warm parts of the ear, the leg pits, the face folds, etc. The more time they spend on the dog, the bigger they become, filling with your pet's blood and becoming as big as a dime. Take your forceps and carefully pull the tick out to make sure you get the pincers. Promptly flush the tick down the toilet or light a match to it. Put alcohol on the wound and a dab of antibiotic salve.

Let common sense, a good veterinarian and knowledge of your dog be your guides in coping with all health problems.

HOME CARE FOR YOUR APBT

Overview

- Be prepared with knowledge about first aid and the items you'll need in case of an emergency.
- You are your dog's dentist. Your veterinarian will likely do an annual tooth-cleaning, but you will care for your dog's teeth in between veterinary visits.
- Know the signs of illness and see the vet right away when something is wrong. Follow his advice for aftercare.
- Your veterinarian will advise you about safe parasite preventatives and how to check for internal and external parasites.

AMERICAN PIT BULL TERRIER

Feeding Your APBT

When planning a feeding program for your APBT puppy, it's best to think "quality" and not "economy." The poor nutritional quality of some of the cheaper dog foods does not provide a fully digestible product, nor do the foods contain the proper balance of the vitamins, minerals and fatty acids necessary to support healthy muscle, skin and coat. Canine nutrition research also has proven that you have to feed larger quantities of a cheaper food to maintain proper condition and health. To keep your APBT in prime condition, feed a quality

Don't forget the water! Dogs need to stay hydrated just as humans do, even more so in the heat and when exercising.

Breeders' Best

dog food that is appropriate for his age and lifestyle. The author recommends that Pit Bull owners consider feeding a top-quality dry dog food manufactured by one of the small specialty companies. Even though these foods can be 2 or 3 times as expensive as the commercial dog foods, their benefits to Pit Bulls is many times that. These foods use only human-grade ingredients with limited additives and include nearly 45% meat products.

Dinnertime for a hungry litter! Breeders are knowledgeable about the best growth-formula foods for the APBT and start the pups out with a quality diet. Most growth occurs in the first year, during which time the optimal diet is essential.

Premium dog-food manufacturers have developed their formulas with strict quality controls, using only quality ingredients obtained from reliable sources. The labels on the food containers tell you what ingredients are in the food (beef, chicken, corn, etc.), listed in descending order of weight or amount in the food. Do not add supplements, table scraps or extra vitamins to the food. You will only upset its nutritional balance, which could affect the growth pattern of your APBT pup and

The APBT's diet is very important. It's the fuel that keeps this athletic dog in top form. Discuss the dietary needs of an active dog with your breeder and vet.

maintenance of your adult. Some "people foods" like chocolate and onions are even toxic to dogs.

There are enough dog-food choices to confuse even experienced dog folks. The major brands now offer foods for every size, age and activity level. As with human infants, puppies require a diet different from that of an adult. The new growth formulas contain protein and fat levels that are appropriate for different-sized breeds. Large-breed, fast-growing dogs require less protein and fat during their early months of rapid growth, which is better for healthy joint development. Accordingly, medium (your APBT) breeds also have different nutritional requirements during their first year of growth.

Don't be intimidated by all those dog foods on the store shelves. Read the labels on the containers. Ask your breeder and your vet what food they recommend for your APBT pup.

A solid education about dog food will provide the tools you need to offer your dog a diet that is best for his long-term health.

If you plan to switch from the food fed by your breeder, take home a small supply of the breeder's food to mix with your own to aid your puppy's adjustment to his new food.

When and how much to feed? An eight-week-old puppy does best eating three times a day. (Tiny tummies, tiny meals.) At about 12 weeks of age, you can switch to twice-daily feeding. Most breeders suggest two meals a day during the life of the dog, regardless of breed. This is especially important for the APBT. Smaller meals, rather than one large one, also help prevent the possibility of bloat, as some theories suggest that gulping large amounts of food or drinking copious amounts of water right after eating can contribute to the condition.

Other bloat-prevention measures include no heavy

Feeding Your APBT

exercise for at least an hour before eating and two hours afterwards. Make sure your dog is not overly excited during meals. It is believed that nervous and overly excited dogs are more prone to this life-threatening condition. Elevate your APBT's food and water bowls.

Free-feeding, that is, leaving a bowl of food available all day, is not recommended. Free-feeding fosters picky eating habits…a bite here, a nibble there. Free-feeders also are more likely to become possessive of their food bowls, a problem behavior that signals the beginning of resource-guarding and aggression. Scheduled meals remind your APBT that all good things come from his owner.

With scheduled meals, it's also easier to predict elimination, which is the better road to house-training. Regular meals help you know just how much puppy eats and when, providing valuable information about your pup's health (changes in his eating habits can signal a problem).

Like people, puppies and adult dogs have different appetites. Some will lick their food bowls clean and beg for

Ways to Ward Off Bloat

Bloat is a condition in which the stomach twists on itself, causing restricted blood flow, shock and death if not treated quickly. Ask your vet about the symptoms and practice simple daily preventatives. Here are some commonsense steps to avoid your dog's swallowing air while he's eating or upsetting his digestion:

- Buy top-quality dog food that is high nutrition/low residue. Test a kibble in a glass of water. If it swells up to several times its original size, try another brand.

- Purchase a bowl stand to elevate your dog's food and water bowls. Dogs should not crane their necks when they are eating.

- No exercise one hour before and two hours after all meals.

- Never allow your dog to gulp his food or water. Feed him when he is calm.

- Place large unswallowable objects in his bowl to prevent him from "inhaling" his food in two mouthfuls.

more, while others pick at their food and leave some of it untouched. Do not overfeed the chow hound. Chubby puppies may be cute, but the extra weight will stress their growing joints. Extra weight may be a factor in the development of hip and elbow disease. Overweight pups also tend to grow into overweight adults who are more susceptible to other health problems.

Always remember that lean is healthy, fat is not. Obesity is a major canine killer. Quite simply, a lean dog lives longer than one who is overweight. Furthermore, think of the better quality of life for the lean dog who can run, jump and play without the burden of an extra 10 or 20 pounds.

Should you feed canned or dry food? Should you offer the dry food with or without water? Dry food is recommended by most vets, since the dry particles help clean the dog's teeth of plaque and tartar. Adding water to dry food is optional. A bit of water added immediately before eating is thought to enhance the flavor of the food while still preserving the dental benefits. Whether feeding wet or dry, have drinking water available at all times, keeping in mind that large amounts of water at mealtimes and gulping water are not good for your APBT.

To complicate the dog-food dilemma, there are also raw foods available for those who

Dog-food manufacturers put much time and research into creating balanced, complete nutrition for the needs of different dogs based on size, age, activity level and special health needs. You must choose the diet that best suits your APBT.

Feeding Your APBT

prefer to feed their dogs a completely natural diet rather than traditional manufactured dog food. The debate about raw and/or all-natural vs. manufactured is a fierce one, with the raw-food proponents claiming that raw diets have cured their dogs' allergies and other chronic ailments. Check with your vet and ask your breeder if you choose to explore this feeding method.

If your adult dog is overweight, you can switch to a "light" food, which has fewer calories and more fiber.

"Senior" foods for older dogs have formulas designed to meet the needs of less active, older dogs. "Performance" diets contain more fat and protein for dogs that compete in sporting disciplines or lead very active lives.

The bottom line is this: what and how much you feed your dog are major factors in his overall health and longevity. It's worth your investment in extra time and dollars to determine the best diet for your APBT.

FEEDING YOUR APBT

Overview

- Quality is a priority in choosing a food for the APBT. Offering a top-quality dog food is the most reliable and convenient way to provide complete nutrition for your dog's health.
- Discuss with your vet and/or breeder a feeding schedule and amounts to feed based on your APBT's activity level.
- Avoid free-feeding, which can lead to picky eaters, obesity or possessive behavior.
- Bloat is a life-threatening condition related to eating and exercise habits that affects deep-chested dogs. Discuss preventatives and symptoms with your vet, and be able to recognize the symptoms so you can get to the vet *immediately* at the first sign.

AMERICAN PIT BULL TERRIER

Grooming Your APBT

Do understand before purchasing your dog that he will need some grooming and attention to his hygiene. However, a big plus with the APBT is that there is a very minimal amount of grooming required, unlike that necessary for a Poodle or some other heavily groomed breed.

A brush with soft to medium bristles is recommended to keep your dog's coat looking shiny and clean. Usually a weekly brushing will do the trick. The brush can be purchased from your

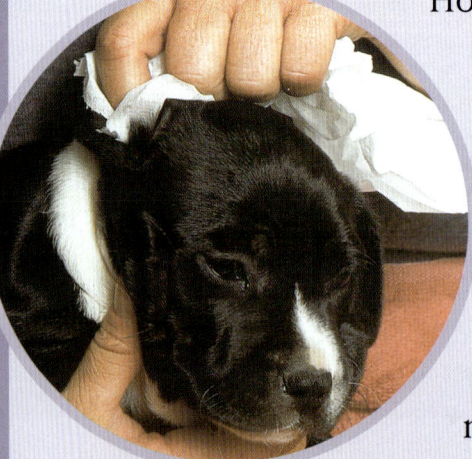

Clean your dog's ears with an ear-cleaning product and a soft wipe or cotton ball. Your local pet shop will have a suitable ear cleaner for you.

Breeders' Best

local pet-supply store. A bath is certainly recommended when your dog is very dirty, but often a rubdown with a damp cloth will be ample for routine cleaning. Frequent bathing will deprive the dog's coat of important oils, drying it out.

It is important to trim your dog's toenails and it is best to start this within a week of bringing him home. Purchase a quality toenail trimmer for pets. You may want to purchase a styptic stick in case you trim the nail too short and bleeding starts. If your dog's toenails are light in color, you will easily see the blood vessel that runs inside each nail. However, it is a bit more difficult to see in dark-nailed dogs and you may nick the blood vessel until you are more familiar with trimming the nails. If you do not start trimming the nails while the dog is young, so that he becomes accustomed to it, you will have greater difficulty in doing so as the

Who says bath time can't be fun? On a warm day, a gentle hosing cools your Pit Bull down and makes him feel much better.

Your APBT's eyes should always be clear and bright and the areas around them kept clean and free of tear stains. Cloudiness in the eye, or any other visible changes, should be brought to your vet's attention at once.

CHAPTER 11

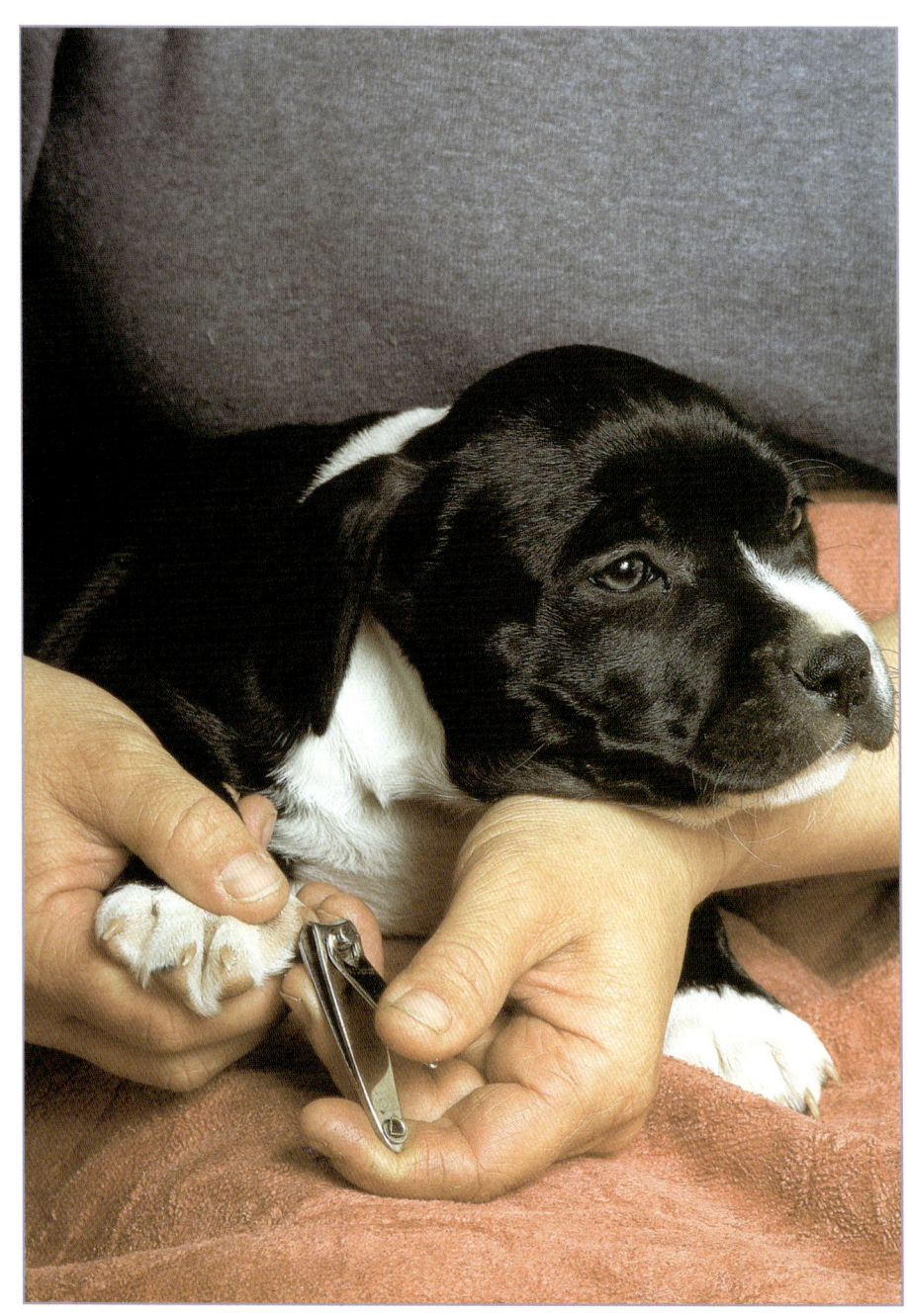

American Pit Bull Terrier

Nail clippers made for dogs make the task easy...well, as easy as possible, since most dogs don't quite enjoy their pedicures!

Grooming Your APBT

Breeders' Best

dog becomes larger, more difficult to hold and more resistant to having his nails clipped.

To wrap it up: this is a "wash and wear" dog...easy to groom. Give him at least a weekly brushing, trim his toenails every month or so, make sure his ears, eyes and teeth are clean and wipe him down with a damp cloth when he looks like he needs it. Give him a bath only when it is necessary. You will now have a clean, good-looking dog that you can be proud to be seen with!

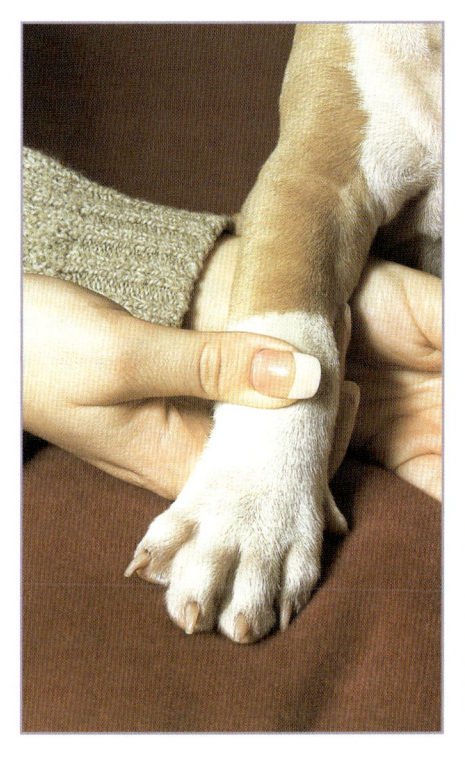

In dogs with light-colored nails, clipping is easier because you can see the vein (called the quick) and thus avoid trimming too close to it.

GROOMING YOUR APBT

Overview

- While the APBT is very low-maintenance as far as grooming goes, proper coat maintenance is a vital part of his overall health and must begin when the pup is young.
- The APBT owner must tend to his dog's coat as well as nails, ears, eyes and teeth.
- You will only have to bathe your APBT occasionally. Wiping him down as needed will keep him clean between baths.
- Your APBT will look great in his sleek, shiny coat.

CHAPTER 12

AMERICAN
PIT BULL TERRIER

Keeping Your APBT Active

Many owners and their dogs are looking for challenging things to do. There are many activities to keep both of you very busy, active and interested. Pit Bulls can excel in many activities because of their intelligence, their willingness to please and their tenacity. After Puppy Kindergarten, you may want to work toward an AKC Canine Good Citizen® award. This is a program that, when successfully

If you set the pace, your APBT will join you, and you will likely tire long before he does!

completed, shows that your dog will mind his manners at home, in public places and with other dogs. This class is available to dogs (pure-bred or otherwise) of any age. It's a fun course and useful for everyday life. There are ten steps, including accepting a friendly stranger, sitting politely for petting, accepting light grooming and examination from a stranger, walking on a loose lead, coming when called, responding calmly to another dog, responding to distractions, going down on command and remaining calm when the owner is out of sight for three minutes. Upon successful completion, your dog will receive an AKC Canine Good Citizen® certificate.

Obedience is a sport at which the APBT can excel. Obedience trials are held either by themselves or in conjunction with a dog show. There are different levels in obedience trials, with each level progressively more

Breeders' Best

Always introduce new activities with encouragement, praise and, of course, a treat! Reward your APBT for learning new things.

Although not one of the sporting dogs, your APBT can enjoy games of fetch as much as any retriever.

CHAPTER 12

American Pit Bull Terrier

difficult. The rules of obedience trials, exercises to be completed and titles that can be earned vary depending on the club hosting the trial. Some typical advanced exercises include off-lead work, silent hand signals and picking the right dumbbells from a group of dumbbells, although the beginning levels are much easier, consisting of variations on basic commands. It is a major accomplishment for both owner and dog when a title at the highest levels of obedience is achieved.

Agility, started in England, is a fairly new sport in America and can easily be observed at dog shows. Look for the large, noisy ring filled with competitors and dogs running through the course, with excited spectators watching at ringside, joining in with cheers.

Dogs are taught to run a

You'd have to see it to believe it! The APBT can easily suspend himself in mid-air by grasping onto a rope with his extraordinarily strong teeth and jaws.

Keeping Your APBT Active

Breeders' Best

course that includes exercise and obstacles like hurdles, ladders, jumps and a variety of other challenges. There are a number of degrees that a dog can earn in agility, again depending upon the hosting club and the obstacles that the dog is able to conquer.

Agility requires good communication between owner and dog. The APBT's athleticism helps him fly through the course! It has become very popular in the US, providing good exercise for owner and dog but, most of all, lots of fun!

In order to excel at any

Encourage your pup to bring the toy back to you, not run away with it!

79

American Pit Bull Terrier

of the activities we've discussed, or any areas of the dog sport for that matter, it is essential to belong to a dog club where there is an experienced trainer as well as equipment and facilities for practice. Find a good school in your area and attend a class as a spectator before enrolling. If you like the facility, the instructor and the type of instruction, sign your dog up for the next series of lessons.

Canine sports have

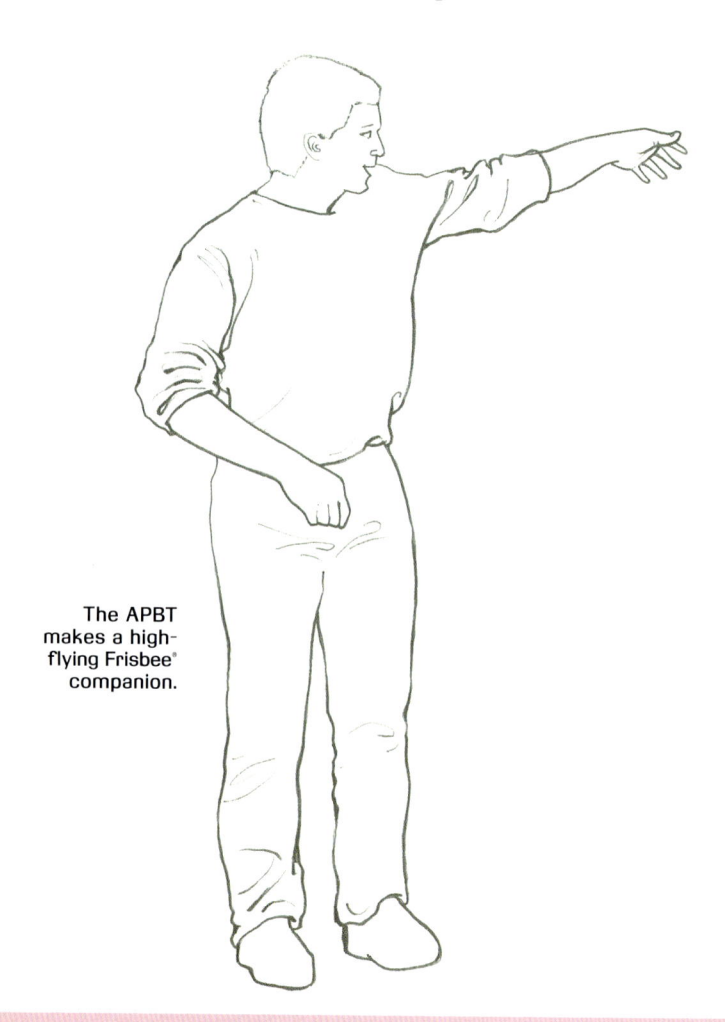

The APBT makes a high-flying Frisbee® companion.

Keeping Your APBT Active

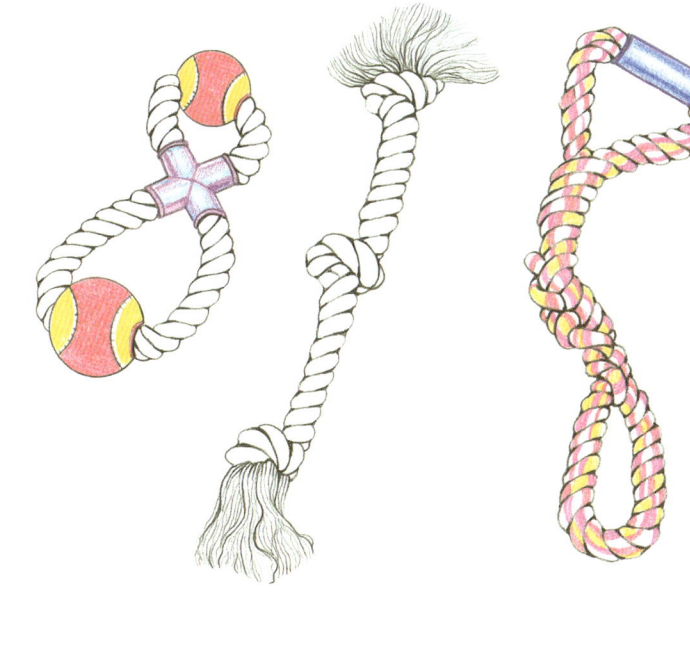

Breeders' Best

Strong rope toys are popular with dogs, and they have the added benefit of acting like dental floss as the dog chews.

become so popular with the public that there should be little difficulty in finding a training facility. You will find it a great experience to work with your dog and meet new people with whom you will have a common interest. Your success will take time and effort on your part, and a willing dog working on the other end of the leash.

Weight pulling is an excellent sport for Pit Bulls, as they like to show off their strength and tenacity. The ADBA holds weight-pulling contests and you can find their locations through the *American Pit Bull Terrier Gazette.* The club will also send you a copy of the rules for weight pulling.

It's a good idea, when using your dog to pull weights, to have a good harness that will fit the dog correctly; otherwise, the dog can damage his shoulder muscles. ABPTs hold world

American Pit Bull Terrier

records for weight pulling in several classes.

Schutzhund is also a sport that Pit Bulls can enjoy and excel at. Started in Germany to determine breeding quality in German Shepherds and eventually other breeds, it is a sport that demands the best from your dog. APBTs are not attack dogs, as some think, but dogs that are trained for courage, intelligence and sound temperaments. When taking up this sport with your dog, it is absolutely essential that you attend a reputable class with qualified trainers.

Of course, the easiest way to keep your dog active and fit is to take him for a walk every morning and evening. This will be good for you, too. Of course, playing games with your dog will delight him. Chasing a ball or tugging on strong rope toys

Carting is an age-old task that has been performed by many breeds; today it is mainly for fun and hobby. What child wouldn't enjoy being "carted" around by his favorite dog?

Keeping Your APBT Active

Breeders' Best

are always great fun for a dog. Pit Bulls have very strong jaws and teeth and you need the most durable of toys to have them last more than one or two play sessions. Never give him a toy or ball that is small enough for him to swallow, as, like a child, he will swallow it and an expensive trip to the veterinarian may follow. Many Pit Bull owners and trainers recommend using treadmills, springpoles and flirt poles to condition their ever-active dogs. For the dog's safety, the owner must know how to use them properly and how to recognize signs of fatigue. Keep in mind also that these devices are regarded as "dog-fighting gear" in some places; check with your local ordinances before investing in this equipment.

Some owners of APBTs and similar breeds use treadmills as a form of exercise for their dogs. The dog treadmill may look odd to those unfamiliar with it, but the dogs seem to love it.

KEEPING YOUR APBT ACTIVE

Overview

- Your active, athletic and intelligent APBT will welcome the challenge of participating in new activities. He is certainly capable of success in many areas of the dog sport.
- Obedience, agility and weight pulling are just a few of the sports open to APBTs and their owners.
- To train for canine competition, join a club where you can get professional instruction.
- Daily walks reinforce that special bond between you and your APBT.
- Your APBT's favorite activities will be things he can do with you.

CHAPTER 13

AMERICAN PIT BULL TERRIER

Your APBT and His Vet

Before bringing your pup home, the breeder may have had certain cosmetic procedures done on the puppy. In America, if the ears are cropped it is done at 9 to 11 weeks of age by a veterinarian who is familiar with the cropping of ears. If the ears are still taped when you bring your puppy home, the breeder will tell you what kind of care to give for proper healing. A note about ear cropping: ear cropping consists of the ear leather's being surgically trimmed. The ear is

Whether your APBT is an "only child" or part of a big pack, be as vigilant with his health care as you are with every family member.

Breeders' Best

then taped to stand upright. Originally, cropping was done to prevent the ears from being bitten by an adversary. With the fighting dogs and terriers, a cropped ear gave the opponent less to hang onto. Some owners like ear cropping for cosmetic purposes, as it gives the dog a very smart look. APBTs may or may not have their ears cropped; it is a matter of personal preference.

Before bringing your dog home, you should find a good veterinarian. Your breeder, if from your area, should be able to recommend someone; otherwise, it will be your job to find a veterinary clinic that you like.

A consideration in finding a veterinarian is to find someone, for convenience, who is within ten miles of your home. Find a veterinarian whom you like and trust and with whom you can be confident that he knows what he is doing. See that the office looks

Puppies get plenty of activity by exploring and playing. Never force or overdo exercise with a young pup, as it can cause stress on his growing frame and contribute to future orthopedic problems.

Many APBT owners today choose to forgo ear cropping with their dogs, as it is purely for cosmetic purposes.

American Pit Bull Terrier

CHAPTER 13

Your APBT will surely spend time outdoors in the grass, so he should be protected from parasites and insects and the diseases that they carry. Discuss preventative measures with your vet.

and smells clean. It is your right to check on fees before setting up an appointment, and you will usually need an appointment unless it is an emergency. If you have a satisfactory visit, take the vet's business card so that you have the clinic's number and the name of the veterinarian that you saw. Try to see the same vet each visit, as he will personally know the history of your dog and your dog will be familiar with him.

Inquire if the clinic takes emergency calls and, if they do not, as many no longer do, get the name, address and telephone number of the emergency veterinary service in your area and keep this information with your veteri-

Your APBT and His Vet

Breeders' Best

One of the first things that you and your new APBT puppy will do together is take a trip to the vet.

American Pit Bull Terrier

narian's phone number.

On your first visit, take along the card that your breeder gave you with a record of the shots that your puppy has had so that the veterinarian will know which series of shots your pup should be getting. You should also take in a fecal sample for a worm test.

The recommended vaccines are for distemper, infectious canine hepatitis, parvovirus infections and parainfluenza. Although this seems like an impressive list of shots, there is one shot that will cover all of these viruses...DHLPP. This series of shots will start between six and ten weeks, which means that the breeder will be giving the first shots to the litter and the vet will have to finish up the series of three shots, given at four-week intervals.

Distemper at one time was the scourge of dog breeding, but with the proper immunization and a clean

Many illnesses and parasites can be passed from dog to dog, but if your dog has received the required vaccinations, beginning in puppyhood, he can enjoy spending time with his canine pals worry-free.

Your APBT and His Vet

Breeders' Best

Start with a healthy puppy and build a foundation for a happy life together. Veterinary care, proper nutrition and training are key elements in a long and rewarding relationship between dog and owner.

American Pit Bull Terrier

puppy-rearing area, this no longer presents a problem to the reputable breeder.

Canine hepatitis, very rare in the United States, is a severe liver infection caused by a virus. Leptospirosis is an uncommon disease that affects the kidneys; it is rare in young puppies, occurring primarily in adult dogs. Parvovirus is recognized by fever, vomiting and diarrhea. This is a deadly disease for pups and can spread very easily through their feces. The vaccine is highly effective in prevention.

The APBT, like other terriers, is considered to be a healthy breed and there are few hereditary problems within the breed. Problems to watch for are undershot bites, excessive bone and muscle in the shoulders, kidney stones and juvenile-onset demodicosis. Kidney stones will be suspected when your dog is drinking an excessive amount of water and/or urinating often. A trip to the veterinarian can diagnose the problem. Your

Protect your pup from common canine problems by following the vet's advice about which vaccinations the pup should receive. Visit the vet on schedule and keep up with booster shots, too.

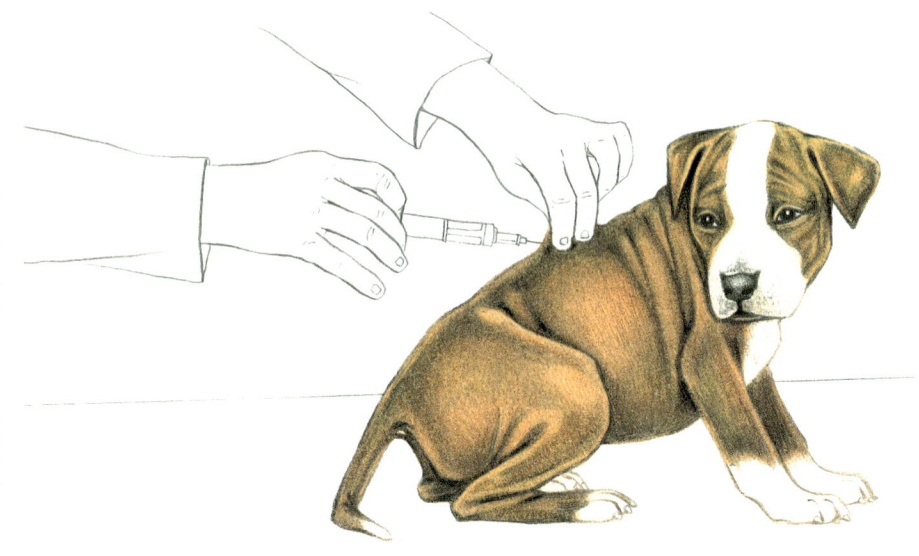

Your APBT and His Vet

Breeders' Best

Alert your vet if you notice any changes in your APBT's toileting habits. More frequent urination can be indicative of various problems.

veterinarian will either try to dissolve the stones or will perform surgery to remove them. The dog will continue to live a normal life, but you may have to keep him on a special dog-food diet to keep stones from reforming.

Juvenile-onset demodicosis occurs in young dogs between 3 and 12 months of age. There will be several localized areas or patches of hair loss and scaling. Common sites are around the eyes, the corners of the mouth and on the forelimbs. The lesions may or may not be itchy for the dog. Your veterinarian will perform

American Pit Bull Terrier

skin scrapings to determine his diagnosis. Treatment will vary, depending upon the severity of the demodicosis. Medication or, more commonly, baths in a special shampoo will be used to clear up the condition.

Perhaps the largest problem with the APBT regarding health and/or wounds is that the Pit Bull is known to have an extremely high tolerance for pain. Thus, torn muscles and ruptured ligaments are common injuries; the dog is really unaware of his own brute strength and thus may not show the extent of his injury.

Health guarantees are important, and a responsible breeder will give you a contract that will guarantee your pup against certain congenital defects. This guarantee will be limited in time to six months or one year. If there is a problem, he will possibly replace the pup

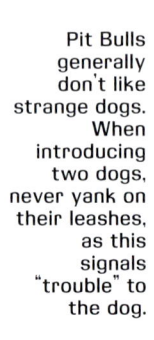

Pit Bulls generally don't like strange dogs. When introducing two dogs, never yank on their leashes, as this signals "trouble" to the dog.

Your APBT and His Vet

Breeders' Best

or offer some refund in his price.

A last note: you may or may not want to consider neutering or spaying your Pit Bull, or the breeder may require this. A neutered male will be less aggressive, less likely to lift his leg in the house and have less of a tendency to mount other dogs (or your leg). A spayed female will not come into season every six months; these seasonal cycles not only are very hard on your house but also will attract neighboring dogs.

Neuter/spay also offers many health benefits for both males and females.

Chew toys contribute to your APBT's good dental health as well as keeping him occupied and out of mischief.

YOUR APBT AND HIS VET

Overview

- If your APBT puppy's ears are cropped, you will need to learn from the vet or breeder how to care for them until healed.
- Find a vet whom you like and trust, and plan on bringing your APBT for a checkup very soon after bringing him home.
- Keep your puppy's scheduled veterinary appointments.
- The breeder should have discussed with you all of the breed's potential hereditary problems and given you a health guarantee for your pup.
- The APBT is slow to show signs of pain.
- Discuss spaying/neutering with your breeder and vet.

CHAPTER 14

AMERICAN PIT BULL TERRIER

Your Aging APBT

As your dog ages, he will start to slow down. He will not play as hard or as long as he used to. He will sleep more. He will find the sunbeam in the morning hours and take a long nap. At this time, you will probably put him on a senior-formula dog food, but continue to watch his weight. It is more important than ever not to let your senior citizen become obese. You will notice that his muzzle will gray. You may see opacities in his eyes, signs of cataracts. And as he becomes older, he may become arthritic.

Take special care with your APBT in his senior years, in return for the many years of happiness he has brought you.

Continue your walks, making them shorter. Give him a baby aspirin when he appears to be stiff. Keep the grooming up, as both you and he will like to have him looking and smelling his best. Watch for lumps and bumps and take him to the veterinarian if problems arise. Incontinence can also become a problem with the older dog. This is frustrating for you and hard on the house, but he hasn't become unhousebroken; rather, the muscle tone of his excretory system is fading.

Terriers are, in general, blessed with long lifespans. They can often be very healthy to 12 to 14 years of age, and it is not unusual for them to live to 15 or 16 years if they have good care.

Veterinary care has changed much over the last decade or two, as has medical care for humans. Your veterinarian can now do much to extend your dog's life if you want to spend

Breeders' Best

APBTs are hardy terriers that remain active and alert for well over a decade.

While younger APBTs never seem to run out of gas, the older dog will need more frequent periods of rest.

Chapter 14

American Pit Bull Terrier

the money. Unfortunately, while this will extend your dog's life, it will not bring back his youth. Your primary concern should be to help your animal live out his life comfortably. There are medications that can be helpful. Whatever you do, try to put your dog, his well-being and his comfort ahead of your emotions. Do what will be best for your pet.

Always remember the many wonderful years that your pet gave to you and your family and, with that thought, it may not be long before you are looking for a new puppy for the household. And there you are, back at the beginning with a cute bundle of joy, ready for many more years of happiness!

You may find that your senior needs to go out more frequently for bathroom visits. Be aware of the changes that accompany aging and accommodate your old friend.

YOUR AGING APBT

Overview

- Be aware of the physical and behavioral changes that accompany old age and be patient with your dog's slower pace.
- Keep things consistent for your senior dog, adapting your routine as necessary to make things easier on your old friend.
- Your APBT, with proper care, will live well into the double digits.
- Your senior dog may need more frequent trips to the vet. The vet can advise you how to care for your APBT so that his senior years will be healthy and fulfilling.